# Gather 'Round the Dinner Fable

Read-Aloud Story Devotions for Families

# Gather 'Round the Dinner Fable

## Steven James

HONOR **HB** BOOKS

*Inspiration and Motivation for the Seasons of Life*

COOK COMMUNICATIONS MINISTRIES
Colorado Springs, Colorado • Paris, Ontario
KINGSWAY COMMUNICATIONS LTD
Eastbourne, England

Honor® is an imprint of
Cook Communications Ministries, Colorado Springs, CO 80918
Cook Communications, Paris, Ontario
Kingsway Communications, Eastbourne, England

GATHER 'ROUND THE DINNER FABLE
© 2006 by Steven James

Cover Design: Greg Jackson, Thinkpen Design, LLC

Published in association with the literary agency of The Knight Agency, 577 South Main St., Madison, GA 30650.

The Web site addresses recommended throughout this book are offered as a resource to you. These Web sites are not intended in any way to be or imply an endorsement on the part of Cook Communications Ministries, nor do we vouch for their content.

First Printing, 2006
Printed in the United States of America

1 2 3 4 5 6 7 8 9 10 Printing/Year 10 09 08 07 06

Unless otherwise indicated, all Scripture quotations are taken from the *Holy Bible, New Living Translation*, copyright © 1996. Used by permission of Tyndale House Publishers, Inc., Wheaton, Illinois 60189. All rights reserved. Scripture quotations marked MSG are taken from *THE MESSAGE*. Copyright © by Eugene H. Peterson, 1993, 1994, 1995, 1996, 2000, 2001, 2002. Used by permission of NavPress Publishing Group; NIV are taken from the *Holy Bible, New International Version®. NIV®*. Copyright © 1973, 1978, 1984 International Bible Society. Used by permission of Zondervan. All rights reserved.

ISBN-13: 978-1-56292-744-8
ISBN-10: 1-56292-744-2

LCCN: 2006926032

For Wayne and Sue,
who listened when that's what I needed most

# CONTENTS

# Acknowledgments

Thanks to Trinity, Ariel, Eden, Liesl, and Esther.

# INTRODUCTION

GOD KNOWS that sometimes the best way to tell the truth is to tell a story. He knows we learn, think, remember, and communicate through stories. And he also knows that telling stories is the best way to impact us for eternity. That's why the Bible is a storybook and not a textbook. And that's why, when Jesus came to fulfill God's promises, he didn't come as a philosopher or a theologian. He came as a storyteller. Mark describes Jesus' teaching like this, "He used many such stories and illustrations to teach the people as much as they were able to understand. In fact, in his public teaching he taught only with parables" (Mark 4:33–34).

Parables, fables, myths, and fairy tales have always been a popular and effective way to share spiritual and moral truth with the next generation because stories connect with both the head and the heart. They fly beneath our radar and move us closer to the place where we can personally encounter the truth. The kid-friendly parables and fables in this book will help you pass along important biblical truths to your children in a fun and engaging way.

I wrote this book because over the years I've found that it's really difficult to locate easy-to-use, fun family devotional books. Many of the ones I've tried to use with my children require too much preparation time (which, for my family, is anything longer than about eighteen seconds). Others depend on elaborate object lessons to be effective, and I don't usually have the necessary Popsicle sticks, ice cubes, marbles, bowling balls, and parachutes on hand. Still others are targeted for kids of a specific age group and don't appeal to a broad range of ages—either my youngest daughter is confused or my oldest is bored. Often I have to rephrase and rewrite the devotions as I read them just to keep my children's attention!

In addition, many devotional books are full of good moral advice but have little to do with Jesus, grace, forgiveness, or the other truths the gospel message is all about. Here's the essence of what they teach: Be nice. But Christianity isn't about creating nice people, it's about creating new people altogether. The gospel is the exciting news of God's undeserved love for us and the explanation of how we can enter the family of God through faith in Jesus Christ.

*Gather 'Round the Dinner Fable* is easy to use and gospel-focused, works with children ages four through twelve, and was written with busy families in mind. The devotions are quick, fun, and teach biblical truth in an imaginative and memorable way.

Each devotion follows the FABLE format:

FIND THIS OBJECT—suggestions for optional object lessons that relate to the main character or concept of the story. (No bowling balls or parachutes here, just common everyday items.)

ASK THESE QUESTIONS—sample discussion questions to help introduce the story or draw lessons from it.

BEGIN THE STORY—read-aloud stories written in easy-to-understand language to snag and keep the attention of children of all ages.

LEARN FROM SCRIPTURE—a Bible verse or short devotional thought that reinforces the theme of the story.

END WITH PRAYER—prayers you and your family can use to apply the main points of the devotion.

Enjoy!

# 1

# THE GREAT WHITE
# STONES OF DEATH

## FIND THIS OBJECT

BUBBLE GUM——Get enough bubble gum for everyone to chew and let people blow bubbles during the story. (Hey, at least it'll help keep them quiet!)

## ASK THESE QUESTIONS

Everyone's afraid of something. Some people are afraid of the dark. Others are afraid of monsters, and still others are afraid of needles, or small places, or snakes, or big brothers and sisters. What are you afraid of? Why? *(Tell about a time when you, the parent, were afraid. What happened?)* Why do you think God lets scary things come into our lives?

## BEGIN THE STORY

Wanda was a piece of pink, juicy bubble gum. She lived in a package with four other pieces of gum—she was the third one from the right.

Even though some pieces of gum are scared of dark places, Wanda wasn't. And even though some gum is scared of small packages, Wanda wasn't. In fact, she was afraid of only one thing—the Great White Stones of Death. Oh, she'd heard stories about them all right!

Sometimes the piece of gum on her left would tell scary stories of what it's like to get chewed—shoved into a dark and squishy cave and then crushed by the Great White Stones of Death.

Ooh … it was horribly frightening.

*I wanna stay right here in my wrapper where it's safe,* thought Wanda. *I wanna stay right here forever!*

But one day a little girl named Emily bought Wanda's package of gum and unwrapped it.

"Oh, no!" cried Wanda. "Without my wrapper I'm naked!" And she would have blushed, but bubble gum isn't able to blush. And she would have covered herself up, but the girl had already thrown Wanda's wrapper away.

Then, the little girl popped Wanda into her mouth.

"Oh, yuck!" yelled Wanda. "It's all wet and soggy and gross in here! And it smells like … pepperoni pizza."

That's when Wanda saw Emily's teeth. They were white and shiny because Emily was a good brusher.

"Oh, no! The Great White Stones of Death!" cried Wanda.

Emily opened her mouth wide.

"Help!" yelled Wanda.

And then Emily chewed. Her teeth pressed down, making Wanda feel very squished and squashed and squooshy. "Ugh! I've got tooth marks on my face!" she said. And then Emily pushed Wanda around with her tongue. "Yuck!" said Wanda. She felt very flat. And wet. And naked. Wanda wasn't happy at all.

But Emily was. "Mmm," she said. "Yummy gum!"

Then Emily pushed Wanda between her teeth to flatten her out, she parted her lips, and began to blow. Wanda felt a great pepperoni-flavored wind push against her. Then she began to stretch and flex and grow.

Emily blew Wanda into a bubble the size of a grapefruit.

"Wee! Look at me!" said Wanda. "I'm the biggest piece of gum in the world! I wasn't scared for a minute! Look how round I am! Look how—"

*Pop.*

Before Wanda could say another word, she burst in the air. Emily giggled and pulled the pieces of Wanda out of her hair and her nose and her ears, and slid them back into her mouth and began to chew again.

But this time, Wanda didn't mind at all. She understood that the Great White Stones of Death were really only there to soften her up so she could do what she was always meant to do—blow incredibly big bubbles. And besides, being in Emily's mouth was much better than being in her nose.

*I guess I don't have to be scared after all,* thought Wanda. *Even though it hurts a little at first, when it's all done I'm big and round and beautiful!*

And, thinking that, she began to grow into a wonderful bubble once again.

## The End

> Hard times, rough times, tough times come,
> Sometimes life just ain't much fun.
> So when you get lonely or scared or sad,
> Remember that God can bring good things from bad.

## LEARN FROM SCRIPTURE

Just because you're a Christian doesn't mean life is always going to be easy. In fact, sometimes life is toughest for believers. But God can turn even tough times into blessings. In the Bible, a man named Paul had lots of hard times. People hurt him and put him in jail. While he was in jail he wrote, "Rejoice in the Lord always. I will say it again: Rejoice! ... Do not be anxious about anything" (Phil. 4:4, 6 NIV).

Another time he wrote, "I consider that our present sufferings are not worth comparing with the glory that will be revealed in us.... We know that in all things God works for the good of those who love him" (Rom. 8:18, 28 NIV).

Sometimes it feels like we're getting crushed and smushed by our problems, and that can be scary. But God is using all those experiences—both the good ones and the bad ones—to shape us into something beautiful. In 2 Corinthians 4:8–9 Paul wrote, "We are pressed on every side by troubles, but we are not crushed and broken. We are perplexed, but we don't give up and quit. We are hunted down, but God never abandons us. We get knocked down, but we get up again and keep going."

And just like Wanda, that's when we're the most beautiful, especially if we continue trusting in God through it all.

# END WITH PRAYER

God, you have a super plan for each of us. Help us to trust you even when it seems like you're smushing us. Help us to remember that you're really just getting ready to do something great in our lives.

Show us how wonderfully you can turn bad things into good ones, hard times into easy times, and rough times into smooth ones. Teach us to accept even the scary times knowing that you want to grow something beautiful in our lives. Amen.

# 2

# THE WORD-EATING GIRL

## FIND THIS OBJECT

YOUR EAR—Examine your ears. Are your earlobes attached or dangling? Are the ears of the people in your family shaped alike? Who has the smallest ears? The squiggliest ones?

## ASK THESE QUESTIONS

When you hear kind words, how does that make you feel? What about when harsh, mean words enter your ears? Words are very powerful and can be used in both good and bad ways. But what if you could not only hear words, but taste them?

## BEGIN THE STORY

Once there was a girl who could swallow the words that she heard. It was a very strange gift. Whenever people spoke to her, she could actually taste what they said on the tip of her tongue as she heard the words enter her ears.

But it wasn't just the words themselves, like if someone said, "rocky road ice cream" or "cheeseburger with mayo." She wouldn't taste the ice cream on her tongue or the meat, and the cheese, and the sesame seed bun, but rather the flavor of how the words were said and what they meant.

So, when her little brother called her "booger brain" or "acid breath," it tasted like hot sauce on her tongue. When she heard mean kids at school calling her names, it tasted like she was swallowing sawdust and tears. And when her daddy held her close and said, "I love you," it tasted like the world's most expensive chocolate truffles melting in her mouth.

And, while she certainly enjoyed the "I love you" words best of all, some of the tastiest words—almost as tasty as the "I love you" words—were the ones she heard but wasn't supposed to. Like when she listened to some of the girls in her class talk about other girls behind their backs. When she heard those words, they tasted sweet and secret and daintily delicious. In fact, they tasted so good that one day she sat and listened to them for almost two hours, swallowing every word and enjoying each of them on the way down.

But later that day, she got a huge stomachache from devouring all that gossip. And the strange thing was, from then on the good words didn't taste quite so good anymore. Even the "I love you" words had lost some of their sweetness. And all she could think about was swallowing more and more dainty morsels of gossip, even though she knew they would give her a huge tummyache in the end.

## The End

Be careful what you listen to, be careful what you hear.
For words can travel to your heart directly from your ear.
And though it may seem sweet at first,
this truth is always true—
Gossip will turn sour once it climbs inside of you.

## LEARN FROM SCRIPTURE

Proverbs 18:8 says, "What dainty morsels rumors are—but they sink deep into one's heart." *(If necessary, explain what gossip and spreading rumors means.)* When you listen to and share gossip and rumors, you end up hurting both other people and yourself. Gossiping about others and spreading rumors is never productive or a positive thing.

God wants us to use our words to build up, not tear down. Let's ask him to help us do that and to forgive each of us for the times we've feasted on juicy pieces of gossip.

## END WITH PRAYER

God, forgive us for the times we've shared dainty morsels of gossip. Help us to avoid listening to and sharing things behind other people's backs. Amen.

# 3

# THE PIG AND THE STORK

## FIND THIS OBJECT

A PILE OF MULTI-COLORED JELLY BEANS, chocolate candies, or gummy bears—Tell the children they can each choose two different candies to have as a treat.

## ASK THESE QUESTIONS

How did you decide which ones to choose? Was it tough or easy to decide? Are there certain foods you never say yes to or never say no to?

Everybody wants to be happy, but many people are not. What are some of the ways people try to become happy? This story will help you think about which roads to happiness you may want to take and which ones to avoid.

## BEGIN THE STORY

Once there was a pig who wanted to be happy. Now, I should tell you, this pig looooved chocolate. He ate chocolate all the time. He would pig out on it. Seriously, he would.

So one day he said, "I'm going to eat as much chocolate as I want! That'll make me happy!" So he did. He ate chocolate for breakfast, chocolate for lunch, and chocolate for dinner. He had chocolate snacks, drank chocolate milk, and had chocolate treats between meals. He even chewed chocolate gum, ate chocolate vitamins, and used chocolate-flavored salad dressing rather than the vinaigrette.

Soon that pig grew to the size of a house, then the size of a gymnasium. He became famous. People came from all over the world and paid lots of money to see him. And with all the money he made, that pig just bought more and more chocolate.

Nearby, there lived a stork who wanted to be happy too. She was friends with the pig, and one day he told her he still wasn't happy even after eating all that chocolate. *Hmm,* she thought. *He must be unhappy because he eats all that chocolate. If I want to be happy, maybe I shouldn't eat any chocolate at all!*

So, when her friends had birthdays, she wouldn't eat any chocolate cake. She refused all offers of chocolate candy. And she would only eat broccoli and beets for her bedtime snack. And when it came time for dessert, she would leave the table and go to the marsh and suck on muddy reeds and rocks. After all, she didn't want to get fat, and mud is low in saturated fat and cholesterol. "I'm never going to eat any chocolate or candy or sweets or ice cream or anything!" she said. "Not ever!" And she didn't. And she grew skinny and stuck-up and eventually got a job in the library telling people to be quiet all day long.

Now the pig was fat and unhappy, and the stork was skinny and unhappy. The pig had said yes all the time, but found no happiness. The stork had said no all the time and became just as unhappy as the pig. So what do you think the secret to true happiness might be?

## *The End*

Saying no all the time isn't very much fun,
Saying yes all the time will get you undone.
Knowing when to say yes and when to say no,
Will help you find happiness wherever you go.

## LEARN FROM SCRIPTURE

God wants us to say yes to his ways and no to sin, but when it comes to other areas of life, moderation is usually the best idea.

Solomon wrote, "Do not be overwicked, and do not be a fool—why die before your time? It is good to grasp the one and not let go of the other. The man who fears God will avoid all extremes" (Eccl. 7:17–18 NIV).

Part of following God is avoiding extreme ways of acting—like never having fun or never being serious; or maybe never enjoying a good meal or never denying yourself anything. A little chocolate is okay, a little mud-covered rock is okay—well, maybe not, but you get the idea. We can learn from both the pig and the stork as we try to follow Christ. He has given us guidelines in his Word to help us stay balanced in life.

## END WITH PRAYER

> God, thanks for caring about us so much that you give us the ability to make decisions. Teach us when to say yes, when to say no, and how to avoid all extremes. Help us to make healthy choices and find our deepest happiness in you. Amen.

# 4

# THE STOLEN BONE

## FIND THIS OBJECT

A RIDDLE——Ask your children if they know any riddles. Usually after one person shares a riddle, someone else will think of one! Spend a few moments trying to figure out riddles as a family. (If you need one to get you started, try this: What can go up a chimney down, but not down a chimney up? Answer: an umbrella.)

## ASK THESE QUESTIONS

When you try to figure out a riddle, usually the answer that you think of at first isn't the right one. Things usually aren't quite what they appear to be. Can you think of other areas of life where that's true too?

## BEGIN THE STORY

A dog named Rufus lived on a farm. One day he was roaming through the fields when he saw his friend, Fang the Wolf, nearby. It looked like Fang was chewing on a nice, meaty bone.

"Hey, Fang!" called Rufus. "What are you gnawing on?"

Fang looked up and grinned. "My new bone, Rufus! It's the best one I've had in months!"

Rufus was curious. "Where did you get it?"

"I stole it from that big dumb German shepherd down the road!"

"What? You stole it!"

"Yeah! And it really tastes great. Try it for yourself!"

So Rufus tasted the bone for himself. But after gnawing on it for a few minutes he shook his head. "Hmm …" he said. "It doesn't taste all that great to me."

"Well," said Fang, leaning over the bone again, "that's because you didn't steal it."

## The End

It seems like sinning will be loads of fun,
But in the end you'll regret it, when it's over and done.

## LEARN FROM SCRIPTURE

When you're tempted to do something you know is wrong, does it seem like it'll be fun or exciting or cool? Usually that's the way things work! But then when you get caught, it's not so much fun anymore. Disobeying might give us a thrill, but it's the wrong kind of thrill. It almost always seems safe to sin at first, but in the end it's never worth it.

Listen to what Solomon wrote about folly (that is, foolishness) calling out to people who lack good judgment, "Stolen water is refreshing; food eaten in secret tastes the best!" That's what foolishness said, but then Solomon adds that the former guests of folly are now in the grave (Prov. 9:17–18).

Proverbs 20:17 gives a similar warning, "Stolen bread tastes sweet, but it turns to gravel in the mouth." Let's hope Fang doesn't choke on that stolen bone! And let's pray that we can be wise and refuse to listen when foolishness and sin call out to us.

## END WITH PRAYER

God, it's tempting to think that we'll have more fun by doing something that's not right. Help us instead to trust that you know what's best for us and then listen to your voice instead of the voice of foolishness. Amen.

# 5

# THE TWO THIEVES

## FIND THIS OBJECT

A WATCH or wall clock with a second hand

## ASK THESE QUESTIONS

I have a question for you. I want you to think about it for the next ten seconds: "What is the most valuable thing you own?" Ready? Get set. Go!

*(Give them ten seconds to think about it.)*

Okay, what are your answers?

*(Allow them to respond.)*

All of those are certainly important and valuable things. In today's story something very valuable has been stolen, but you may be surprised to find out what it is.

## BEGIN THE STORY

Once there were two thieves who worked together. One would distract people out on the street while his friend would sneak into their homes and steal clothes from their bedrooms! Socks, shirts, pants, even underwear! One day, they were both caught and taken to the judge.

"Which of you did the stealing?" asked the judge.

"Um, I did," said one of the men.

"You actually stole their underwear?" said the judge.

"Um, once in a while."

The judge shook his head and pointed to the other man. "And you distracted the people?"

He nodded.

The judge thought for a moment and then said to him, "So, how did you do it? Tell me about it."

The second man smiled, thinking the judge was going to let him go since he hadn't stolen anything. "Well, Your Honor, I would ask people about the weather, talk about sports scores, compliment them, and say whatever I could to hold their attention, while that man over there took their things. Socks. Shirts. Pants—"

"Yes, yes, I know," said the judge. "And underwear."

"You see, Your Honor, I never actually stole anything myself."

"You just distracted people?" said the judge. "By wasting their time?"

"That's right."

The judge cleared his throat. "All right then, here are your sentences: The one who stole the clothes must return them and give each person an extra piece of clothing in addition to the ones that he took. And buy them some new underwear."

The first man nodded as his sentence was announced. "Yes, Your Honor." It wasn't a very serious sentence at all.

Then the judge continued, "The other man must go to prison for the next ten years."

"What!" cried the lawyer representing the second thief. "But Your Honor! I don't understand! Why would you give such a harsh sentence to my client? After all, he just wasted people's time! He never even committed a crime!"

The judge replied, "His crime was greater! I gave these sentences because the first thief stole something that could easily be replaced—people's clothes; but your client stole something that can never be repaid—people's time."

## The End

It may not seem like a terrible crime,
But it's the worst kind of stealing
To waste someone's time.

# LEARN FROM SCRIPTURE

Do you agree with the judge's decree? Why or why not? What sentence would you have given the men? How does this story help you to understand the importance of how you spend your time?

When you waste people's time, you actually cause them to waste part of their life. After all, wasted time is wasted life. When you make people wait for you or selfishly refuse to do your share of a job or assignment, you're stealing something that can never be repaid. For example, watching TV instead of packing your lunch might make the whole family late to school or to work. Or, choosing to finish your video game while everyone waits at the dinner table for you is a waste of other people's time.

Each day, each moment, is a precious gift from God. As Psalm 118:24 says, "This is the day the LORD has made. We will rejoice and be glad in it." Let's do that right now.

# END WITH PRAYER

God, forgive me for the times I've stolen people's time without even realizing it and for the times I've wasted the moments you've given to me. Help me to be more aware of how precious every moment is. Amen.

# 6

# DANIELLE'S DEBT

## FIND THIS OBJECT

SOMETHING VALUABLE THAT MIGHT BREAK—Talk about how much the valuable item cost or how hard it would be to replace if it were broken. What would happen if you were messing around and you accidentally broke it?

## ASK THESE QUESTIONS

Did you ever owe somebody money for something and not have enough to pay them back? How did that make you feel? If you break something that belongs to someone else, who pays for it? What if you don't have enough money?

## BEGIN THE STORY

Once upon a time there was a sixth-grade girl who was playing a full-contact version of Tackle the Wannabe Future Homecoming Queen in the living room with her friends and accidentally smashed her dad's priceless collection of ceramic turtles, imported directly from eastern India, right as he came through the door.

"Oops," she said. "This is not a good thing."

"That's my priceless collection of ceramic turtles imported directly from eastern India!" shouted her father.

"Um, yeah, well, I'll pay you back, Dad." She said. "I promise!"

He stared at the pieces of ceramic turtles scattered across the floor and then sighed. "You can't even afford a bag of gummy bears from Wal-Mart. There's no way you can afford a priceless collection of ceramic turtles imported directly from eastern India." As soon as he realized his daughter would never be able to pay for the turtles, out of the kindness of his heart he said, "Danielle, you don't owe me anything. I forgive your debt. I'll pay for the turtle collection myself."

"For real?"

"For real."

"Cool!"

"But don't play that Tackle the Homecoming Queen game in the living room anymore."

"It's called Tackle the Wannabe Future Homecoming Queen."

"Whatever. Don't play it in the house."

"Um, okay."

At first Danielle felt thankful that her dad had forgiven her, but then she started to feel bad about him having to pay for the ruined collection himself. After all, she was the one who'd broken the turtles. *Hmm,* she thought. *Maybe if I pay him back then I won't feel so bad. Yeah, that's what I'll do! I'll earn some money to pay him back so I won't feel indebted to him. Then we can call it even!*

So she worked hard all around the house folding clean clothes, mowing the lawn, and even giving sponge baths to their pet lizard, Fido. Her mother paid her for all of those chores, and when she'd earned $2.39, she brought it to her father.

"What's this for?" he asked.

"To pay off my debt," Danielle said.

"What debt?"

"The one I owe you for the turtles."

"But that was cancelled," he said. "You don't owe me anything. You can't repay what you don't owe. Keep your money."

"But—"

"Go on, you can keep it."

So Danielle kept the money, but she still felt weird about it. She kept doing odd jobs around the house, some of them odder than others, all the while thinking, *This time he'll accept it because it's more money than before.* But once again when she brought the money to her father, he refused to accept it. "You don't owe me anything!" he said. Then he looked at her kindly. "Danielle, you keep bringing me this money. Why? Is it out of guilt or out of love?"

Danielle didn't know what to say. "I'm bringing it to pay you back for smashing the priceless collection of ceramic turtles imported directly from eastern India!"

But her father shook his head. "Then I can't accept it. Your debt was cancelled long ago. You don't owe me anything."

This went on for a long time—Danielle trying to repay her father, her dad refusing to accept the money—until one day she realized he really *didn't* want her to pay him back at all, and that every time she brought the money to him, she was doing it for herself and not for him.

As soon as she understood this, Danielle rushed to her father with all that she'd earned and saved up. "Here, Dad!" she said, dropping it all at his feet.

"Why are you bringing me this?" he asked again.

"Out of love, Daddy!" she said. "Because you cancelled my debt! And since I don't owe you anything I want to give you everything!"

When he heard that, he threw his arms around her. "At last you understand!" he said. "At last! At last!"

And as far as I know, Danielle and her dad and the new ceramic turtle collection are living happily ever after.

## *The End*

Forgiveness means debts are forgotten and gone,
Like grass that's been mowed in the middle of the lawn.
They're snipped back and cut down and no longer grow.
You cannot pay back what you no longer owe.

## LEARN FROM SCRIPTURE

Have you ever felt weird when someone forgives you for something? Ever felt like you needed to pay them back to even the scales? We sometimes act like that toward God. But when you finally realize you don't owe anything, you're free at last to give him all of yourself.

When Jesus talked about forgiveness, he often spoke about it in terms of debts that have been cancelled. The wrongs that we do, the sins that we commit, become like a great big debt that we owe God and can never repay, no matter how hard we try. That's why Jesus paid for our sins with his life.

Jesus once told a story about two people who owed a debt (see Luke 7:41–43). One man owed lots of money, and the other man only owed a few pennies. Neither had enough money to repay their debt, so the man they'd borrowed the money from, out of the kindness of his heart, cancelled both of their debts.

Then Jesus asked one of the people listening to his story, "Which of those men do you think loved that guy more?"

What do you think?

That's right. When someone forgives us, we fall more in love with them.

So if that's true, why do you think the father finally accepted his daughter's money in the end? If the girl didn't owe him anything, why did she offer him all that she had? How will this story help you follow Jesus and express your love for him?

## END WITH PRAYER

God, you have cancelled a debt that's even more costly than a priceless collection of ceramic turtles imported directly from eastern India. Help us to finally realize that we can't repay you. Help us respond with the love and thanksgiving that only come from knowing we're truly free and completely forgiven. Amen.

# 7

# THE BIG FREEZE

## FIND THIS OBJECT

A REFRIGERATOR/FREEZER—Open and close the doors of your refrigerator and freezer; let your children stick their hands inside. Discuss which one is colder.

## ASK THESE QUESTIONS

What's the hardest part about living in a family?

Why is it so easy to get into arguments?

Imagine if a refrigerator and a freezer didn't get along. What problems might they have? What things might they argue about?

## BEGIN THE STORY

Frosty and Geri just didn't get along, and whenever the Richardson family went away on vacation, it only got worse.

"You're a wimp!" yelled Frosty the Freezer. "I'm stronger because I'm colder!"

"You're so cold and mean no one can live with you!" said Geri the Refrigerator.

"Humph!" said Frosty.

"Humph!" said Geri. She preferred to be called "the Refrigerator" rather than "the Fridge" because it sounded more sophisticated. She was rather stuck up that way.

Frosty the Freezer shook his head (which was actually his door). "I'm stronger, and I'll prove it!" And then, Frosty puffed out clouds of air so cold the temperature in the kitchen dropped ten degrees. "Beat that!" said Frosty.

"Why would I want to?" Geri knew she could never be as cold as Frosty, so instead she began to warm herself up. She opened her door and let all her cool air out. But soon, the yogurt inside of Geri began to spoil and the cheese began to sweat. "See how nice and toasty warm I am?" she said.

"And stinky," said Frosty. "That yogurt is nasty."

As you can imagine, that just made things worse. The more Frosty puffed and the more Geri opened her door, the tippier they became until—CRASH!

They both fell to the floor together and all the food inside of them spilled out. The linoleum was covered with mayonnaise mixed with pickles ... and ice cream mixed with ketchup ... and cherry-flavored Popsicles resting on pieces of soggy broccoli. Neither Geri nor Frosty was strong enough to pull themselves upright again. So when the Richardson family finally *did* get back from vacation, they found a huge stinking, rotting mess in the kitchen.

"Whew! Yuck!" said Mrs. Richardson. "It smells like spoiled yogurt and moldy meat!"

"Gross!" said her ten-year-old daughter.

"Cool," said her twelve-year-old son.

"Oh, well," said Mr. Richardson, patting Geri and Frosty. "I guess this old thing must have just shorted out. I suppose it's time to get a new fridge, anyway."

"I'm a refrigerator!" said Geri, "not a fri—!"

But before she could finish, Mr. Richardson had walked over to the wall. Both Frosty and Geri watched as he reached for the plug.

"Uh-oh," they said at the same time. Then, they didn't say anything at all because they weren't plugged in anymore. And Mr. Richardson took them to the dump and bought a new refrigerator and freezer that weren't nearly so argumentative. And his electric bills went down considerably too.

## The End

Arguing and bragging usually make a big mess.
So think of others a bit more and yourself a bit less.

## LEARN FROM SCRIPTURE

We all know we're supposed to get along, so what makes it so hard? *(Let everyone respond.)* Usually, the tough thing isn't knowing what we're supposed to do, but actually doing it. That's why Paul wrote to the Christians in the city of Philippi who were having a tough time getting along:

> Is there any encouragement from belonging to Christ? Any comfort from his love? Any fellowship together in the Spirit? Are your hearts tender and sympathetic? Then make me truly happy by agreeing wholeheartedly with each other, loving one another, and working together with one heart and purpose.
>
> Don't be selfish; don't live to make a good impression on others. Be humble, thinking of others as better than yourself. Don't think only about your own affairs, but be interested in others, too, and what they are doing. (Phil. 2:1–4)

That's good advice. It's the comfort of God's love that has the power to help us get along with each other. What's one way that we can start living out this verse in our family this week? Let's ask God to help us do that right now.

## END WITH PRAYER

God, help us get along better and not get on each other's nerves so much. When we're tempted to argue and fight, remind us that it usually doesn't solve anything, but only leads to more trouble. Let your Spirit guide us and your love change us. Help us to plug in to you and stop worrying so much about being better than anyone else. Amen.

# 8

# LEAVING THE CAVE

## FIND THIS OBJECT

A FLASHLIGHT—Turn off the lights and read this story with a flashlight. Crawl under the table together if you want.

## ASK THESE QUESTIONS

What would it be like to live in a cave all the time? It might be fun at first, but after awhile it would get rather wet and cold and clammy. Today's story is about some people who chose to live in a cave, and never, ever left.

## BEGIN THE STORY

Once upon a time, a fierce dragon was terrorizing the land. He would appear when people least expected him, burn down their homes, and attack and eat their livestock. First, he would breathe fire on their cattle; then he would gobble them up because he really loved roast beef. Yummy.

Well, since the dragon was so dangerous, the people moved out of their homes and into the caves that dotted the nearby countryside.

Living in the caves made the people dirty and grouchy and didn't help their eyesight one bit. It was wet and dark in the caves and sometimes bats would hang upside down from the people's earlobes like great, black, wriggling earrings. But the people put up with the darkness and the dampness and the batty earrings. "If we go outside the cave," they said, "the dragon will burn us up or eat us alive! Roast people! Yuck!"

One day, a visitor came to the caves. He went from one cave to another telling the people that they could come out because the dragon had been killed. "The prince has slain him!" he cried. "Come back to your homes and join the celebration that the king is putting on!"

He went from cave to cave spreading the good news. He showed people the dragon scales that the prince had given to him. He even showed them a decree signed by the king declaring a day of feasting and dancing in honor of the prince.

A few people believed the messenger. They climbed out of the caves they'd been hiding in for so long and ventured into the daylight once again. It was a little scary at first, since they'd become so used to the darkness, but when they left the caves at last, the bats flew away and stopped hanging from their earlobes. So that was cool.

But most of the people didn't leave. "We don't believe you," they told the messenger. "We're going to stay right here where the dragon won't get us."

"But the prince has already conquered him!" said the messenger.

"Go away!" they said. "We're staying right here. We don't want to be roasted alive."

When the messenger realized he couldn't convince them, he went to join the king's victory party. The people who hadn't believed him stayed there in the dark, damp caves with bats hanging from their earlobes, all because they refused to believe that the dragon had been slain.

And only the ones who left the caves lived happily ever after.

## *The End*

Let's pray ...

> God, the darkness around us is gloomy and deep,
> So often our souls are fast asleep.
> Wake us up from our slumber in this terrible night
> And lead us into freedom with the news of the light.

## LEARN FROM SCRIPTURE

Would you have left the caves or stayed there with bats hanging from your ears? What was the difference between those who stayed and those who left? Can you think of anything this story teaches us about our relationship with God?

Peter reminds us that God has "called [us] out of the darkness into his wonderful light" (1 Peter 2:9). And when Paul was writing to the believers in the early Christian church about God's power, he reminded them: "He has rescued us from the dominion of darkness and brought us into the kingdom of the Son he loves, in whom we have redemption, the forgiveness of sins" (Col. 1:13–14 NIV).

*(If necessary you may wish to explain that to be "redeemed" means that you have been bought back again. As the New Living Translation puts it, "God has purchased our freedom with his blood and has forgiven all our sins" [Col. 1:14]. This would also be a good time to invite your children to become believers if they have never done so by asking, are you still stuck in the dark, or have you believed the message and left the cave?)*

Who in today's story do you think represents the Devil? Who would represent Jesus? What about you—are you in the cave or have you left the cave to join the victory celebration?

## END WITH PRAYER

*(Turn on the lights in one room and leave the lights off in another room. Take turns stepping from the darkness and into the light as you thank God for loving you, freeing you, and rescuing you by defeating the ancient dragon so long ago.)*

> God, your story is powerful enough to bring us freedom and new life. Help me to believe in you with all of my heart and then join you in the victory celebration. Amen.

# 9

# A JOB FOR GRAY

## FIND THIS OBJECT

THINGS THAT ARE GRAY—Have a two-minute scavenger hunt to see if your children can find three things that are gray. Go.

## ASK THESE QUESTIONS

What is your favorite color?

What's the most important color of all? Why do you say that? What makes you think so?

Which colors are in the rainbow? Which ones aren't? If colors had feelings, how do you think the ones left out of the rainbow would feel? Today's story is about one of the colors you don't usually see in the rainbow.

## BEGIN THE STORY

None of the other colors liked Gray.

He was just too depressing to be around. I mean, he was the color of fog and winter and the outside of an elephant's ear—not exactly the cheeriest things in the world.

But Red on the other hand—Red was a very popular color! So bright and lively and on fire for everything! And then there was Blue—calm, reasonable, and deep like the ocean. Green was as lush and beautiful as a springtime meadow or the leaves of the forested hills. And Brown, well, he was the color of worms and dirt, and you can imagine how that made him feel.

But even Brown laughed at Gray. "You're just a mixture of Black and White!" he would say. "Why, you hardly even look like a color at all!" Yes, even Brown was more popular with the other colors than Gray.

Sometimes the other colors called Gray names that I shall not repeat. And they told him that he was the most boring and bland and un-fun color of all. That was actually the word they used—un-fun. For, although they were mean, they were not very clever when thinking up insults.

And after awhile, Gray began to believe them. *I must be the most useless and miserable color in all the world*, thought Gray. *And un-fun, too.*

So he began to hide, sometimes in the shadows of ancient boulders, and sometimes in the corners of the clouds or in the heart of the autumn rain. He hid so well that the other colors began to leave him alone and eventually forgot that he was there.

But since Gray was hiding, the clouds in the sky had no texture; they were either completely white or totally dark. Cement sidewalks began to disappear, and skateboarders started crashing into trees, or riding on grass or dirt. And at circuses all around the world, elephants began to turn invisible, which terribly frightened all the four-year-old girls with pigtails.

Several months passed before the angel in charge of rainbows came looking for Gray. "Where's Gray?" he asked the other colors.

"How should we know?" they said. "He hasn't been around in ages."

"Gray!" called the angel. "Come on out! I need your help!"

Gray slowly stepped out from behind a raindrop. "Yes?"

"God sent me to find you," said the angel. "He needs someone to color the hair and crown the heads of the wisest people in the world. Of course, White does all right, but she could use your help making people look distinguished. And besides, there's plenty of hair to go around … except on some of those men. Anyway, come on. You'll become known as the mark of maturity and wisdom!"

"Really?" said Gray. "Not the guy who's un-fun?"

"Really," said the angel. "And God also wants you to go back to the clouds, the sidewalks, and the elephants. They all miss you. You're making four-year-olds cry."

"Oh. Sorry," said Gray.

"It's all right. But it's time to get back to work."

"Okay," said Gray.

So Gray stopped hiding and began to live in the hair of the three wisest groups of people in the world—doctors and teachers and kindly old grandmothers.

After that, the other colors left Gray alone. They realized he must be quite important since God had sent the rainbow angel to give him a special job. And they didn't call him un-fun anymore, either.

By the way, the next time you see someone with gray hair, be sure to tell him, "You look *very* distinguished." And I'll bet he'll smile and thank you. And even though you may not see it, Gray will smile and thank you too because he has finally realized what an important color he really is.

## The End

Every color, every shade, every evening hue,
Is important to God just like me. Just like you.
Finding our purpose and finding our place
Is part of the privilege of living in grace.

## LEARN FROM SCRIPTURE

If God came looking for you, what special job do you think he might assign to you? What would you say to him if he did? Would you say yes or no?

God created lots of different colors and shades of colors. Did he have to? Then why do you think he did it? What does that tell you about God? Does it tell you anything about why there are so many different kinds of people in the world? Explain what you mean.

In the Bible, Paul compared Christians to a body, in which each part—each person—serves a different, unique, and important role: "All of you together are Christ's body, and each one of you is a separate and necessary part of it" (1 Cor. 12:27).

*(If you wish, you could read through 1 Corinthians 12:12–27 to further explore Paul's analogy and its application to today's story.)*

# END WITH PRAYER

God, help us remember that each one of us is important in your eyes. We each have a unique job and special place in the world. Help us to never look down on other people whose role is different from ours, even if they might at times seem un-fun to us. Amen.

# 10

# MOUSE AND SNAKE

## FIND THIS OBJECT

YOUR TONGUE—Take turns sticking out your tongues at each other! Then, play a game of tongue tag: the person you stuck your tongue out at does so to someone else. (No, don't really tag them with your tongue!) Be silly about it. Have fun.

## ASK THESE QUESTIONS

Sticking out your tongue is usually considered rude and it's meant to hurt someone's feelings. How does it make you feel when someone says something mean to you or does something to purposely hurt your feelings? Can they usually make up for it just by saying, "I was only joking!" when it's all over? Why doesn't that seem to help?

Remember that as I read this story about Mouse and Snake.

## BEGIN THE STORY

Mouse was sitting on a log when she saw Snake slithering along on the forest floor. Since she was on the log, she figured she was safe and called out, "Hey there, Mr. Snake! There's something I've been meaning to tell you!"

"What'sssss that?" hissed Snake, looking up in her direction.

"You sure are one ugly fellow!" she said.

"Come down here and ssssssay that."

"I think I'll stay right here!" replied Mouse, smirking. Then, to show she wasn't scared at all, Mouse did a little dance up there on the log. But as she did, her foot slipped and she tumbled off the log and landed right next to Snake's mouth.

"Now, Mousssssse," he said with a grin, "what was that you were sssss-saying?"

"Um ... what a handsome fellow you are?" squeaked Mouse.

But Snake just smiled. "You can't make up for one insult—even with a hundred complimentssssss. I'm going to eat you up, not for the compliment you just gave me, but for the insult you gave me at firsssssst."

And you know what? That's just what he did.[1]

## The End

Words can be good or they can be rotten,
But either way, insults aren't easily forgotten.

## LEARN FROM SCRIPTURE

Do you think Snake was right when he said, "You can't make up for one insult—even with a hundred complimentssssss"? What do you think this story can teach us about the things we say and the words we use? How will this story change how you treat the rest of your family?

When you say something, it's like shooting an arrow through the air. You can't just take it back after you've said it because once it's in the air, it'll hit the target even if you immediately wish you hadn't released it. It's too late to take it back.

That's why the Bible says, "Like a madman shooting firebrands or deadly arrows is a man who deceives his neighbor and says, 'I was only joking!'" (Prov. 26:18–19 NIV). And Proverbs 12:18 reminds us, "Some people make cutting remarks, but the words of the wise bring healing."

One last thing, Snake wasn't very forgiving, was he? The Bible tells us to forgive as we have been forgiven (see Eph. 4:32). Is there someone who has said something mean to you whom you need to forgive? Will you forgive them now, as we pray?

# END WITH PRAYER

God, it's easy to say unkind words. Help me to be more careful with the things I say and the words I use. And when people hurt me by the things they say, help me to forgive them just as you have forgiven me. Amen.

# 11

# The Lumberjack's Gloves

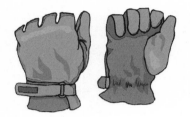

## Find This Object

A PAIR OF GLOVES OR MITTENS—You may want to lay the gloves on the table or wear them the whole time you read the story. It might even be fun to get a pair for everyone to wear and have a silly time eating your whole meal wearing gloves or mittens!

## Ask These Questions

Why do we wear gloves? How strong are gloves all by themselves? How much can gloves accomplish when they're not being worn?

## Begin the Story

Once upon a time there was a pair of leather gloves that belonged to a lumberjack. The left glove was named Ted; the right glove was named Todd. The lumberjack wore his gloves all through the forest as he hauled lumber, cut down trees, and carried his axe and saw around the woods.

One day Ted and Todd were lying on the lumberjack's bunk where he'd left them while he went to eat a great, big, heaping pile of blueberry pancakes for breakfast.

"Ah, I love being so powerful!" said Ted.

"And I love being so brave!" said Todd. And soon, Ted and Todd began to tell Jill the Pillow all about their many adventures.

Jill was so impressed by the amazing tales of the little gloves. "Oh, my!" she said. "You're so strong! Carrying logs around like that!"

"Yup," said Ted.

"Like they were nothing," said Todd.

"And brave! Grabbing saw blades and not even fearing that you might get ripped!"

"Yup," said Ted.

"Never even crossed my mind," said Todd.

"Oh, do show me something!" cried Jill. "Show me how brave and strong you are! Lift me up! Twirl me around! Throw me up toward the ceiling!"

"Well, I usually wait for the lumberjack—" said Ted.

"Me, too," said Todd.

"Oh, come on!" begged Jill. "Show me how powerful you are!"

Ted and Todd were quiet for a moment, and then Ted finally responded. "Um, I don't feel like it right now."

"Me neither," said Todd. "Maybe later."

Then Jill the Pillow understood. "Oh," she said. "I see. So you're not all that strong after all. You can't even pick up one of my feathers without the lumberjack, can you?"

"I could if I wanted to," said Ted.

"Me, too," said Todd.

"Yeah, right," said Jill. Then she turned her back to them both and wouldn't talk to them anymore. Instead, she started talking with the lumberjack's teddy bear named Ricardo who didn't brag nearly so much, and at least he knew he was only stuffed.

## The End

By ourselves the power we have is small;
We can't often do mighty things at all.
But part of the secret in God's big plan,
Is that when his Spirit lives in us, we can!

## LEARN FROM SCRIPTURE

Lots of times we take the credit for the good things God does through our lives. But without his power working in us, we'll never be able to do any mighty deeds. Jesus once told his followers that without him they could do nothing (see John 15:5). And in the Bible it says, "It is not that we think we can do anything of lasting value by ourselves. Our only power and success come from God" (2 Cor. 3:5). It's humbling to admit that, but it's the first step to letting God use us. The power to do good things comes from God. Let's ask him to slip us on and use us in mighty ways, right now.

## END WITH PRAYER

*(If you wish, put on a pair of gloves and think of five good things God has given you the power to do. Share them with your family. Then, ask God to give you the strength to do five more things!)*

> God, fill us up with your Spirit and remind us that without your power working in our lives we will be powerless in all the ways that really matter. Amen.

# 12

# STEPHANIE'S SONG

## FIND THIS OBJECT

HAVE A WHISTLING (or yodeling) contest! See who can whistle the loudest, prettiest, weirdest, and fastest. Or have everyone join together in singing a favorite song. Encourage everyone to join in, even if they don't think singing is really their gift.

## ASK THESE QUESTIONS

What's more important—being skilled at something or trying your best at it? What's the difference? Which requires more courage?

We all know that some people are better at certain things than other people. Should we just stick to the things we're good at? Why do you say that? How will we find out what we're truly good at if we don't try new things? It takes a lot of courage to do our best at something, even though other people are lots better at it than we are. That's what this story is all about.

## BEGIN THE STORY

Stephanie the Sparrow did not have a very pretty voice. In fact, sometimes when she sang, it sounded like an injured water buffalo yodeling old Beatles tunes. Other times it sounded like a lovesick moose calling for his

girlfriend, and once in a while Stephanie's singing sounded like the screech-
ings of a seven-year-old hyena who had just stepped on a nail.

When the other birds heard her sing, they would fly away or groan or
start singing as loudly as they could to try to drown out Stephanie's song.
"Stephanie!" they'd shout. "You stink at singing! Why don't you do us all a
favor and just be quiet!"

"But I like to sing!" said Stephanie.

"Well, we don't like to listen!" said her friends.

And they said it so much that finally Stephanie decided they might be
right. *I guess I just won't sing anymore*, she thought. *Instead, I'll just listen to
the songs of the pretty-sounding birds.*

So Stephanie was quiet. She stopped singing and just listened. At first,
the other birds were very thankful. But then, when Stephanie stopped
singing, the other birds noticed that a robin named Robin didn't have all
that beautiful of a voice, either. They quickly pointed this out to her, just to
be helpful, of course, and it wasn't long before she stopped singing too.
Then they noticed a nightingale named Dale couldn't sing so well, either …

And so it went. One by one, the birds without beautiful voices stopped
singing, and the forest grew quieter and quieter. Soon, even the birds with
pretty songs stopped, for in the silences of the forest, they began to doubt
the beauty of their songs too.

One day, Lion, the king of all the animals, came to visit the forest. "Why
is it so quiet here?" he demanded. "I want to hear some beautiful music!"

But the birds were afraid he wouldn't like their songs, so none of them
sang. They waited for a bird with a more beautiful voice to go first, but no
one sang. That didn't make the king happy at all. "I want you birds to sing
for me!" he said. "Now, sing!" But everyone was quiet. All the birds waited
for the most gifted birds to go first.

"I said, 'Sing!'" roared the Lion. The birds began to tremble, for Lion was
not known as the most patient of the animals. And he did have rather big teeth.

As the silence seemed to grow deeper and more uncomfortable all
around them, the birds heard the sound of an injured water buffalo yodeling
"Yellow Submarine."

"I said I wanted to hear *birds* sing, not large, hairy, tone-deaf mammals!"
Lion bellowed.

"But look!" someone yelled. "It's not a large, hairy mammal, it's Stephanie
the Sparrow!"

"Whoa!" said Lion. "She sounds like a seven-year-old hyena who just stepped on a nail. Someone else sing something quick!"

And they did. All of them did, because Stephanie really was a terrible singer. And the forest became filled with beautiful music once again as all the birds, even those whose voices were not all that pretty, joined in the song. And Lion nodded, "Now that's more like it!" And the birds breathed a sigh of relief.

But remember, they wouldn't have sung at all unless Stephanie had been brave enough to sing before the king, even though her voice was less than perfect. And that's why the animals in that forest still say ...

## The End

> It's courage, not talent that you need to bring;
> A little talent may be all that you need.
> For if only the most gifted birds would sing
> The forest would be awfully quiet indeed.[2]

## LEARN FROM SCRIPTURE

Stephanie had the courage to be heard, to do what was asked of her. Sometimes courage is more important than talent.

God doesn't give us all the same talents or gifts, but he does give each of us what we need to best serve him. Just because we're not as good at something as someone else doesn't mean we can't still use those abilities to serve God and to bring joy to others. We shouldn't be afraid or ashamed to give our all, even if it's not as good as someone else's.

There's a great Bible story about a man named Gideon who didn't really seem like a great warrior or anything, but he was willing to step up and be used by God. And God used him to win some mighty battles (see Judges 6—7).

Jesus' friend Peter wrote to the Christians long ago, "God has given gifts to each of you from his great variety of spiritual gifts. Manage them well so that God's generosity can flow through you" (1 Peter 4:10). Let's ask him to help us do that today.

## END WITH PRAYER

> God, give us courage to use our gifts to make the world a more beautiful place. Remind us that even if we're not the strongest or best or prettiest we still have an important place in your song. Amen.

# 13

# THE VINES

## FIND THIS OBJECT

SOMEONE ELSE'S HAND—Try working together to tie someone's shoes using the right hand of one person and the left hand of another. Don't get too frustrated with each other!

## ASK THESE QUESTIONS

Do you keep going when you face a problem or an obstacle, or do you pull back and give up? If you keep going, what keeps you going? If you give up, why do you give up?

## BEGIN THE STORY

"Why are you climbing that dead tree?" called one vine to the other. "Can't you see it's just a piece of old rotten wood? You'll get all the way up its trunk and it'll fall over on top of you!"

"Dead or alive, why should I care?" said the other. "I'm a vine! I'm a vine! So I climb!" And soon, she had made it to the top of her dead hollow tree. Slowly, she spread out into the leafless branches.

"Fool!" said the first vine. He climbed the healthiest tree he could find and fingered his way out into the branches. But in time, he choked out the sunlight and his tree died.

Then one summer day, a thunderous storm brought both trees crashing to the ground.

The vine who had killed the healthy tree grumbled. "I give up! It's not worth it! I chose a healthy tree and you chose a dead tree and we both ended up on the ground. Life's not fair! It's not worth the effort of climbing! If I'm just going to end up down here again, I'm gonna stay right here on the ground!"

But the other vine began climbing the first tree she came to, saying, "I'm a vine! I'm a vine! So I climb!"

## The End

To climb, to climb is what matters you see.
To climb, to climb, is the thing.
You may end up on the ground again;
You may end up in a sling.
But though you fail and though you fall
And though you want to quit—
A vine is made to climb. It is not made to sit.

## LEARN FROM SCRIPTURE

What do you think this story can teach us? Which vine did you like better? Which one do you think had the better attitude? Attitude has a lot to do with how we understand success.

God doesn't ask us to be successful, just faithful. Lots of times it's easy to get discouraged and want to give up. It's helpful to remember that honest effort is its own reward. Sometimes hard work pays off, and sometimes it doesn't. It's best to enjoy the process either way, staying focused on faithfulness. To those who remain faithful to him, despite bad times, God will give a crown of life (see Rev. 2:10).

The vine climbed because it was a vine. We serve God because we are his servants. That's reason enough.

## END WITH PRAYER

God, help shape our attitudes more by who you are and who we are
than by the good or bad things that happen to us in our lives. Amen.

# 14

# RANDY THE SIREN

## FIND THIS OBJECT

HAVE A WHINING CONTEST to see which child can make the most annoying whining sound. Use a sentence such as this: "But I don't wanna go to bed!"

## ASK THESE QUESTIONS

Who is the best whiner in our house?
  What prize should we give him/her?
  In real life, do you ever get rewarded for whining?
  Sometimes when we don't get what we want, we whine about it. And sometimes whining bugs people so much that they end up giving us what we want just so we won't annoy them anymore! Raise your hand if you whine sometimes. Raise your hand if it sometimes works. Raise your hand if you think it's a good thing to do. With that in mind, let's start today's story.

## BEGIN THE STORY

*(When Randy whines, read his part with a really annoying, whiny voice.)*
  Randy was the newest member of the siren family. His dad had been

an ambulance siren and his mom, a police siren. Randy wanted to work on a big red fire truck some day. But rather than squeal like his mother or blast like his father, Randy just whined all the time.

"I wanna be on a fire truck!" he'd say. "And I wanna do it now!"

"Please stop whining, Randy!" said his mother.

But Randy whined even louder, "But I wanna be on a fire truck!" Again and again and again he whined. His mother just sighed. And Randy kept right on whining. He whined when he was hungry. He whined when he was tired. He whined when he wasn't hungry or tired but just because there wasn't anything else to whine about.

His father pulled him aside one day. "Randy," he said, "if you whine all the time, no one's going to want to play with you or hire you for a job! You have to know when to make your sound and when to be quiet. By whining all the time, you're just driving everyone else crazy!"

"I don't care!" whined Randy. "I don't wanna be quiet! I wanna be on a fire truck!"

"Oh, brother," said his dad, shaking his head.

One day, the fire chief began looking for a new siren. "Hmm, this one seems good and loud!" he said when he heard Randy whining. So he put Randy on his big red fire truck. But Randy wouldn't stop whining, even when there was no fire to go to.

"I wanna go to a fire!" whined Randy. "And I wanna do it now!"

"How do you shut this thing off?" said the fire chief. None of the fire-fighters could sleep at night because Randy was whining all the time, and people in the neighborhood started getting confused because they thought there was a fire even when there wasn't one.

At last, the fire chief had had enough. He took Randy off the fire truck and threw him into a dumpster, where Randy whined for a while before the guy from the fish market tossed a big pile of stinking garbage on his face.

And no one ever heard Randy the Siren whine again.

## The End

To whine isn't kind, and to whine isn't good;
It annoys everybody in the neighborhood.
Though it might seem to work, it's always best
To respectfully ask when you make a request.

## LEARN FROM SCRIPTURE

Well, what do you think this story teaches us? Part of growing up is trying different ways of asking for what we want. Some methods of getting your way are good methods, and some are bad ones. Whining, complaining, and grumbling all the time may seem to work at first, but in the end, they'll all backfire. They're not very good ways to make requests.

In the Bible, the Israelites complained and whined to God a lot while they were traveling through the desert. Bad things happened to them when they did (see 1 Cor. 10:1–11).

Let's learn from Randy and from the Israelites, and let's ask God to help us stop whining, grumbling, and complaining by thinking about all the good things he has done for us instead.

## END WITH PRAYER

God, help us not to whine or complain so much, but rather to speak with gentleness and respect. And please forgive us for all our whiny times. Amen.

# 15

# THE PERFECT TREE HOUSE

## FIND THIS OBJECT

BLANKETS, PILLOWS, AND CHAIRS——Make a fort out of blankets, chairs, and pillows. Have fun working together as a family. Then climb inside it to read today's story. (Or if that's too much trouble, just sit underneath the table and pretend you're in a tree house!)

## ASK THESE QUESTIONS

Some people try to do everything perfectly. Do you know someone like that? Are they good students? Is it easy or hard for them to relax and have fun?

What's one good thing about trying to do things perfectly? What's one not so good thing about trying to do everything perfectly all the time? Keep that in mind as I read today's story.

## BEGIN THE STORY

One day Mr. Franklin told his children, "I'm going to build you a tree house in the backyard!"

"Cool," said Eric.

"Awesome," said Andrea.

Then their father smiled. "It'll be the best tree house in the world!" he said.

"All right!" said the kids.

Mr. Franklin bought some wood and brought it home and began to work on the tree house. Eric and Andrea couldn't wait to play in it! After a few days, they walked outside and it looked to them like the tree house was almost done. "Wow, Dad! It looks great!" said Andrea. "Can we play in it now?"

"It's not quite ready yet," said their father.

"Are you sure?" said Eric. "It looks finished."

"I haven't added electricity yet!" replied their dad. "Just be patient."

"Okay," said the kids, and they went back to the living room to watch TV.

Mr. Franklin worked on that tree house all summer. He spent evenings and weekends working on it. Sometimes his kids would ask him to play catch, but he didn't have time. After all, he was building them the world's best tree house!

Sometimes he had to put in extra hours at work to earn money to pay for all the materials for the tree house. He had to find some way to pay for the revolving doors, the sun roof, and the wraparound deck with the inset whirlpool.

And whenever the kids would come outside and ask him if he was almost done, he would say, "Not quite yet, but be patient! This is going to be the best tree house in the world!"

"That doesn't matter so much to us, Dad," said Eric.

"We just wanna play in it," added Andrea.

"Don't worry," said their dad. "I'll be done soon! Just wait a little longer!"

Two years, three weeks, and eleven days later he burst through the door to the living room. "At last it's finished!" he announced. "The tree house is done!"

"Shh," said Andrea. "I'm trying to talk on the phone!" Then she took her cell phone into the other room to finish talking to her friend Stacy.

"What about you?" said Mr. Franklin, turning to his son. "C'mon! I'll show you around. It's really cool!"

"I'm too old for a tree house," said Eric. "Tree houses are for babies."

"Oh," said Mr. Franklin, slowly. He thought for a moment and then he said, "Well, maybe we could at least play some catch?"

"Naw, I'm not really interested," said Eric. "After all, I never learned how to play baseball."

Just then Andrea stepped back into the room and hung up the phone.

"What about you?" asked Mr. Franklin. "Want to play some catch with me?"

"No thanks," she said. "I'm gonna meet Stacy at the mall."

So Andrea headed out to the mall and Eric sat down to watch TV and Mr. Franklin just stared out the window at the perfectly empty tree house.

## *The End*

Though families might have problems and strife,
Spending time together is vital in life.

## LEARN FROM SCRIPTURE

What important things in the story did the dad lose sight of? A priority is something that we put first in our lives; priorities are the things that are important to us. What was the dad's priority in the story? Can you think of a better priority for him to have had? Can you think of a time when you've mixed up your priorities? Anyone want to tell us about it?

There's a saying: "If you try to do everything perfectly, you'll never get past brushing your teeth." Sometimes when we try to do one thing perfectly we lose sight of other things that are even more important. Some people worry about food, money, cars, toys, or video games, or even tree houses. Jesus knew that might happen to us. That's why he reminded his followers to seek first God's kingdom and make serving him our number one priority.

As Jesus said, "Your heavenly Father already knows all your needs, and he will give you all you need from day to day if you live for him and make the Kingdom of God your primary concern" (Matt. 6:32–33). Loving God and our family are the two most important things—the biggest priorities of all.

## END WITH PRAYER

God, teach us to always put the most important things first in our lives—our faith, our family, and our friends. Remind us to set the right priorities. Then, give us the wisdom and courage to let your priorities shape our goals. Thanks, God. Amen.

# 16

# MRS. FURBLEY
# SURE IS STRANGE

## FIND THIS OBJECT

A PRESENT, a bow, or some wrapping paper—Talk a little about the different types of gifts we might receive. If you want, give each of your children a stick of gum, a penny, or another small gift.

## ASK THESE QUESTIONS

Grace means getting something good that you didn't earn and don't deserve. It's like receiving a present. How do you feel when someone gives you a present? Does it change how you feel about yourself? Does it change how you feel about the other person? Today's story is about a surprising present that came from a very unexpected source.

## BEGIN THE STORY

*(Feel free to change the age of the students in this story to make it closer to the age of your children.)*

Nobody wanted to get Mrs. Furbley for their fifth grade teacher. Everyone said she was as mean as a Texas rattlesnake in a stinky boot on a sunny day.

Well, okay, not everybody said that, but everybody did say she was mean. Some people said she was the meanest teacher in the world!

Everyone wanted to get Mr. Bindle instead because he was nice, like a fluffy little bunny. He never yelled and he let students get away with talking in class, shooting spitballs across the room, and even cheating on their spelling exams. Not Mrs. Furbley, though. She was strict.

One afternoon, both fifth grade classes were being disrespectful and running down the hallway after class.

"Oh, well," said Mr. Bindle. "I wouldn't want to tell them what to do or how to act. After all, I'm only their teacher."

Not Mrs. Furbley though. She announced that her students would have to stay in for recess and write, "We will not run in the hallway," one hundred times each. The kids all groaned and finished up their math problems. A few minutes later the recess bell rang.

But just as they sat down to begin writing their sentences, Mrs. Furbley told them they could go outside to play, and that she would stay inside and write their sentences for them.

"You're going to take our punishment for us?" the stunned class asked.

"That's right," said Mrs. Furbley. "Go on now. I'll see you at the end of recess."

Then she sat down to write 3,200 sentences in twenty minutes.

When the kids from her class got to the playground, the students from Mr. Bindle's class were shocked to see them. "We thought you had to stay inside and write sentences!" they said.

"Mrs. Furbley stayed in to write our sentences for us," said the other kids.

"But why?" asked their friends. "Why on earth would she do that? It doesn't make any sense!"

And they shook their heads. "We don't know. We can't figure it out. But it doesn't seem like something the meanest teacher in the world would do, does it?"

"No, it doesn't," said Mr. Bindle's students. And from then on, they wished they were in Mrs. Furbley's class too, even if they wouldn't admit it out loud.

## The End

To ignore the rules and pretend they're not there
Isn't right or just or good or fair.
But to take the punishment someone else deserves,
Takes a ton of love and guts and nerves.

## Learn from Scripture

Which teacher would you rather have—Mrs. Furbley or Mr. Bindle? Why do you think Mrs. Furbley stayed in to write those sentences for her class? Is it possible to be strict enough to uphold the rules and at the same time kind enough to care about others? Explain what you mean.

Mrs. Furbley was strict but kind. Even though she hadn't done anything wrong, she took upon herself the punishment her students deserved. Does that remind you of anyone? *(Allow them to respond.)* That's right. Jesus did that for us.

As Peter wrote, "He personally carried away our sins in his own body on the cross so we can be dead to sin and live for what is right. You have been healed by his wounds!" (1 Peter 2:24). Sometimes we can learn lessons about God's grace from the most unexpected places.

## End with Prayer

God, teach us what grace is really like. Help us to better understand both your anger over the wrong things we do, and your loving forgiveness toward us. We're sorry for the times we've hurt you. Thanks for taking our punishment on yourself. Amen.

# 17

# THE CAT'S ADVICE

## FIND THIS OBJECT

WATCH A COMMERCIAL on TV, hold up a piece of junk mail, or print out a kid-appropriate piece of spam on the computer.

## ASK THESE QUESTIONS

When you see a commercial on TV or read an ad in a magazine, do you ever stop to think why it's there or what the people who paid for it want? What are the people who made the ad trying to get you to do? Think about it. Are they trying to get you to do something that's good for them, or good for you? What makes you say that? As you listen to today's story, think about the messages you receive and what they are trying to convince you to do.

## BEGIN THE STORY

"C'mon out of that hole," called the cat to the mice. "It's so much better out here! It's bright and beautiful, not so dusty and dark and scary. C'mon out and play with me! You'll be free to run around and enjoy yourself."

Baby mouse heard the soothing words of the cat and asked her mother, "Can I go, Mom? Please? It must be better out there in the light than hiding here in the darkness! It sounds like so much fun!"

But the mother mouse shook her head. "No, my dear. You must always remember that those who offer advice do not always do so with your best interests in mind."

And so the baby mouse stayed in the hole with her mother, and the cat went searching for another mouse hole, thinking, *That's okay. It won't be long before I eat my supper.*

And you know what?

It wasn't.

## The End

Commercials and promises are sweet, of course,
But always remember to check the source.
For things may sound good—too good to be true,
But is the promise-maker really looking out for you?

## LEARN FROM SCRIPTURE

Sometimes people promise you great things. When they do, it's good to ask yourself if they're doing it because it'll be good for you or if it's only good for them.

Jesus once told his followers, "Look, I am sending you out as sheep among wolves. Be as wary as snakes and harmless as doves" (Matt. 10:16). To be wary means to be careful.

People don't always want what's best for you. Jesus told his followers to be careful, but he doesn't want us to become mean and untrusting either. Can you think of one or two practical ways we can remain both careful and innocent?

As it says in the book of Proverbs, "Only simpletons believe everything they are told! The prudent carefully consider their steps" (Prov. 14:15).

The good news is that Jesus is always trustworthy, and when the Bible says something we can trust that God is telling it to us for our good.

## END WITH PRAYER

God, help us to discern your ways in the world, and to learn when to trust people and when to be careful. Give us wisdom so that we make decisions that build up your kingdom instead of leading us into the enemy's traps. Amen.

# 18

# THE BOY WHO CRIED "PIZZA GUY!"

## FIND THIS OBJECT

A RULER

## ASK THESE QUESTIONS

Talk about the ways you use a ruler. Can you trust rulers to tell you the truth? Why do you say that? What good would a ruler be if it lied twice for every time it told the truth? What are some of the reasons people don't tell the truth? Can you think of any good reasons not to tell the truth? Can anyone give me some really dumb reasons not to tell the truth? As you listen to this story, think about whether or not Joey got what he deserved.

## BEGIN THE STORY

*(Feel free to insert the names of other local college or pro football teams.)*

One evening during football season, Joey's dad invited a bunch of his friends over to watch the Tennessee Volunteers whup the Florida Gators. "Now, Joey," he told his son, "you can watch the game with us if you do one special job—"

"But I don't like football!" Joey complained.

His dad thought for a moment. "Hmm, okay, then you can sit upstairs and play video games while we watch the game in the basement if you do the job. Okay?"

"All right!" said Joey. "But what's this job you want me to do?"

"I want you to let us know when the pizza guy gets here. We're going to have the volume on the TV turned up loud, and we're not going to be able to hear the doorbell ring."

"No problem."

"But don't interrupt us until he gets here. Don't cry 'pizza guy!' unless you see the pizza guy."

"Okay. Got it."

So Joey's dad went down to the basement with his buddies, and Joey sat upstairs playing Alien Blastazoid. Once in a while he could hear the men cheer when the Volunteers scored, or groan when the Gators had a good play. But soon Joey got bored being upstairs all by himself blowing up aliens, so he went to the basement door and pounded on it. "Pizza guy!" he yelled. "The pizza guy is here!" He heard cheers from the basement and then someone turned down the game and his dad called, "How much is it gonna cost?"

"Um, come on up and see!" said Joey.

Joey's dad jogged up the stairs and went to the front door. He looked outside but there was no one there. "Um, Joey?"

"Yeah, Dad?"

"Where's the pizza guy?"

"He's not here yet."

Joey's father did not look happy. "He's not here yet?"

"Um, no. Wanna play video games with me?"

"Joey, why did you interrupt the football game and yell 'pizza guy!'?"

"I guess maybe I was bored or something."

"Look, don't cry 'pizza guy!' unless you see the pizza guy! Got it?"

"Yeah."

"You sure?"

"Yeah, Dad. I'm sure. I got it."

Then his dad went back downstairs and Joey blew up aliens for a little while. Soon he became bored again. He ran to the basement door once more and called downstairs, "Pizza guy! The pizza guy is here!" Once again he heard cheers from the basement, and then someone turned down the game and his dad called, "Are you sure this time?"

"Um. Yup! C'mon up!"

And this time, rather than just his dad, the whole pack of hungry men came tramping up the stairs to get some pizza.

But there was no pizza, because there was no pizza guy.

Joey's dad pulled out his wallet and walked over to the front door. He opened it up. "Joey," he said. "Where is the pizza guy?"

"Um, he's not here yet. Wanna play Alien Blastazoid?"

All the men groaned at the same time. "C'mon," one of them said. "Let's go back downstairs! There's no pizza here, *again*!"

Joey's dad was trying not to yell, but he was angry. "I told you, Joey! Don't cry 'pizza guy!' unless you see the pizza guy! Got it?"

"Okay," said Joey.

"Are you sure?"

"I'm sure."

"Because we're trying to watch the game down there."

"I know."

"Okay?"

"Okay."

Then his dad stomped back downstairs and slammed the door just as the pizza guy arrived.

Joey heard the doorbell ring and ran to the front door. "I'll be right back," he told the pizza guy. "I gotta go get my dad. He's got the money."

Then Joey went to the basement. "Pizza guy!" he yelled. "The pizza guy is here!"

But the men downstairs didn't turn down the volume on the game. Instead they turned it up. "We're tired of your little pranks!" someone yelled. "Go back upstairs!"

"No, the pizza guy is really here!" said Joey.

"Shh!" said one of the men. "We're trying to watch the game!"

Meanwhile, the pizza guy grew annoyed standing there waiting around on the porch. He tried the doorbell a few more times, but no one came. Finally, he just shook his head, looked at his watch, and took the sixteen pizzas Joey's dad had ordered and headed to his next stop. After all, he didn't want to be late getting to that house too.

"I'm telling you the pizza guy is really here!" said Joey.

At last Joey's dad sighed. "He better be, Joey, because if he's not I'm sending you to bed without any supper." And Joey's dad came upstairs and opened up the front door and there was no one there.

Joey's eyes got really big. "He was there! He really was!"

"Yeah, right," said his dad. "Just like the last two times, huh? It isn't nice to lie, Joey, especially when there's pizza involved." Then he sent Joey to bed with nothing to eat while he and his buddies ate some chicken wings that he found in the freezer and was able to microwave during a commercial. But the men were not happy about missing out on their pizza.

And to make things worse, the Tennessee Volunteers lost to the Florida Gators by twenty-one points.

## The End

Telling the truth is the best thing to do
Especially when others are counting on you.

## LEARN FROM SCRIPTURE

Why do you think Joey said the pizza guy was there when he hadn't arrived yet? At first he probably thought it was funny, but I'll bet he didn't think it was so funny when he had to go to bed without any supper! Do people begin to trust you more or trust you less when they find out you haven't been telling them the truth?

*(If you want to help your children make the connection between this story and Aesop's famous fable about "The Boy Who Cried Wolf," say, "This story is based on an old, old story about a boy who was in charge of watching over some sheep. Do you know that story? Can you tell it to us?")*

Jesus *is* the Truth and always *tells* the truth. He even explained one time that the devil is the "father of lies" (John 8:44). Let's ask God to help us walk in the truth and speak the truth as we follow the Truth.

## END WITH PRAYER

*(Take turns telling God true things about your life. You can pray some of them quietly in your head if you don't think other people need to hear them.)*

God, we know you love the truth and hate lies. Help us to be honest and caring and not let lies slip in where they're not supposed to. Amen.

# 19

# WALDO'S TRIP
# TO THE SEED STORE

## FIND THIS OBJECT

A PACKET OF SEEDS (OR A POTATO)

## ASK THESE QUESTIONS

Pass the packet of seeds around the table and then ask the children what kind of plants will grow from these seeds. Are you sure? How can you tell?

Today's story has to do with planting and growing the right kind of seeds.

## BEGIN THE STORY

Waldo walked into Pumpernickel's Seed Store and looked around. "I'd like to grow some pumpkins, Mr. Pumpernickel!" he said.

"Ah! A good choice! The pumpkin seeds are right over here!"

"Nope," said Waldo, walking over to the rack of tomato seeds. "I think I'll use these instead!"

"Those are tomato seeds."

"I know."

"They grow tomatoes, not pumpkins."

"Well, *I'm* gonna use 'em to grow pumpkins!" said Waldo.

Mr. Pumpernickel shook his head. "Look, son, pumpkin seeds grow pumpkins. Tomato seeds grow tomatoes. And watermelon seeds grow—"

"Asparagus!" shouted Waldo. "Good idea! I'll take some of those watermelon seeds, too, so that I can grow some nice yummy asparagus!"

Mr. Pumpernickel said, "Am I on one of those hidden camera reality shows you see on TV?"

"TVs grow radios," said Waldo, smiling.

Mr. Pumpernickel's voice was getting louder now. "The kind of fruit you grow depends on the seeds you use! Vegetables come from vegetable seeds! Just like animals! Tigers come from tigers. Octopuses come from octopuses-pi, um, whatever. Walruses come from—"

"Alligators!" shouted Waldo.

"Go away," said Mr. Pumpernickel. "You're crazy in the head."

"Okay," said Waldo. "Right after I buy some of these tomato seeds! They'll make some fine pumpkins, indeed!"

Then he bought those tomato seeds, as well as a few packets of watermelon seeds so he could grow some yummy asparagus. Mr. Pumpernickel shook his head as he watched Waldo leave and said, "I should have become a dentist like my mom wanted."

He closed up the cash register, sighed, and went back to work.

## *The End*

There's a saying in the Bible that's a good one to know—
"The things that you reap are the ones you will sow."
For the seeds that you plant in the ground down below
Will determine the fruit that is going to grow.

## LEARN FROM SCRIPTURE

Can you grow asparagus from watermelon seeds? Can you grow pumpkins from tomato seeds? Can you grow joy by planting seeds of anger? What about growing love by being mean?

The Bible reminds us over and over that the type of things we plant in life will be the kind of things we harvest in life. So if we have stinky, whiny, fussy attitudes, we're not going to grow a whole lot of peace and love in our lives or in the lives of others. As the Bible says, "Don't be misled.

Remember that you can't ignore God and get away with it. You will always reap what you sow!" (Gal. 6:7).

Let's ask God to help us change the types of seeds we plant into the kind that he wants us to grow.

## END WITH PRAYER

God, help us to plant seeds of kindness and sharing. Forgive us for the times we've planted seeds of meanness and envy. Remind us that whatever we plant we will grow. Amen.

# 20

# THE PEARL MERCHANT

## FIND THIS OBJECT

A PEARL or a piece of jewelry with a precious gem in it—Let your children hold the jewelry or try it on. Talk about where it came from and how valuable or precious it is to you.

## ASK THESE QUESTIONS

To buy something valuable, we often have to sacrifice things that are not so valuable or important. Have you ever done that? Have you ever had to give up something that was important—like watching TV, maybe—to spend time doing something that was even *more* important—like practicing shooting baskets or studying for a history test?

Today's story is about something precious and what different people were willing to give up to get it.

## BEGIN THE STORY

One day a pearl merchant named Louie burst through the door to his home. "Guess what, dear!" he called to his wife, Moesha. "I just found the world's greatest pearl for sale at the marketplace! It's as big and round as a melon!"

She put her hands on her hips and raised her eyebrows. "Humph. Well, I don't believe you!"

"Believe me! It's perfect, and I want to buy it!"

"And how are we supposed to afford something like that?" she said.

"Well," said Louie, "I was thinking if we just sold everything we own, we could easily afford—"

"Sell everything we own?!" interrupted his wife. "You've been pearl diving too deep again, Louie. You're as nutty as a pistachio!"

"I'm telling you it's worth it. You should see that pearl!"

Moesha just scoffed. "Nothing could be that valuable!"

"But—"

"We're not selling everything we own just to buy some stupid pearl!" yelled Moesha. "It wouldn't be practical or sensible. And what would the neighbors think?"

Louie the pearl merchant was quiet for a moment. After all, even though he was sure the pearl would be worth it, he didn't want to argue. Finally, he said, "Okay, dear. Whatever you say."

So Louie and Moesha didn't sell anything but continued living in their nice house, in their nice neighborhood, and continued to be highly respected by all the other members of the local country club.

Meanwhile, another pearl merchant saw that pearl of great price and put everything that he owned up for sale so he could buy it. When Moesha heard about it, she just shook her head. "He's crazier than you are!" she told Louie. "Wait, I have an idea! Let's buy his stuff! We can probably get a great deal!"

"But, are you sure?" said Louie.

"Of course!" she replied. "He's a fool to sell everything he owns, and we'd be fools not to buy it all!"

Louie thought about it for a moment. "Well, I guess so," he said at last. And so that's what they did.

"What a great deal!" said Moesha as she and Louie packed up all of their friend's stuff.

"Yeah," said Louie as he watched his friend walk away with that pearl of great price. "What a great deal." And only one person in this story lived happily ever after.

## The End

To enter God's kingdom makes you rich, not poor.
Those who give up all will gain even more.

## LEARN FROM SCRIPTURE

Who do you think lived happily ever after—Louie, Moesha, or the guy who got the great big pearl?

Jesus often talked about how precious the kingdom of God is. Once he told his friends a story about a pearl merchant. He said, "The Kingdom of Heaven is like a pearl merchant on the lookout for choice pearls. When he discovered a pearl of great value, he sold everything he owned and bought it!" (Matt. 13:45–46). What do you think Jesus wanted his followers to learn from this story? We can't buy our way into heaven, so what do you think Jesus was emphasizing when he talked about selling or giving away everything we own?

To enter God's kingdom means to believe and follow him, and then live by the guidelines of God. Jesus often told people that to follow him they would need to give up everything else. Many people don't realize how precious it is to know and follow Jesus. How much would you be willing to give up to become closer to Jesus? A little? A lot? Everything? It's a good question, not just for people of Jesus' time, but also for us today.

## END WITH PRAYER

God, the most precious thing of all is to enter your story. Remove whatever might be getting in the way between us and you. Amen.

# 21

# MRS. DOOPALAPOOZY AND THE GREAT DESK INSPECTION

## FIND THIS OBJECT

A CEREAL BOWL OR COFFEE CUP—Smear the inside of it with mud or dirt. Then, hold it up so the children can't see the inside. Discuss whether or not it's clean. Then, show them the inside of it.

## ASK THESE QUESTIONS

Can you tell if something is clean just by looking at the outside of it? Why or why not? What are some things that look clean on the outside but aren't clean on the inside? Keep that in mind as I read today's story.

## BEGIN THE STORY

Mrs. Doopalapoozy cleared her throat and said, in her typical teacher voice, "All right, class. I want each of you to clean your desks! We are going to have something called an 'inspection'—which means I'm going to check to see how clean everyone's desk is!"

All the fourth grade students quickly shoved everything that was on top of their desks inside of their desks. And Mrs. Doopalapoozy began her inspection. She walked up to Caliph's desk first.

"Look how nice and clean my desk is!" bragged Caliph.

"Very nice," said Mrs. Doopalapoozy. "Now open it up."

Caliph gulped. "Um, open it, what?"

"I want to see how clean it is inside."

"But, I thought—"

"Open it up."

By now all the other kids were staring at him. He took a deep breath. "Okay, if you say so."

And Caliph opened his desk up all the way. Piled in among his books were math assignments that he was supposed to have turned in three months ago, fifteen notes about PTA meetings he never took home to his parents, a snake skin he'd found on the way to school one day, four pencils he'd never quite gotten around to sharpening, three broken erasers, two bottles of glue that had tipped over and seeped out, and a partridge in a pear tree.

"What's with the partridge?" asked Mrs. Doopalapoozy. "And how did you fit that pear tree in your desk?"

"Small root system," said Caliph. "And the partridge is good at science. He sometimes tutors me."

"AWK!" said the partridge.

"You have got to be kidding," said Mrs. Doopalapoozy.

"Um," said Caliph, "when you said, 'Clean your desk,' I thought you just meant the outside. And mine's very shiny out there, see?"

Mrs. Doopalapoozy just shook her head. "What's more important, Caliph, the outside or the inside?"

"Um … the outside?"

"No, Caliph, the inside! The outside is just what people see. The inside is what matters most."

"Oh," said Caliph. "I was hoping maybe it was the outside."

"AWK!" said the partridge.

Mrs. Doopalapoozy sighed. "Look, I want the inside of your desk cleaned by lunchtime or you're going to have to stay in for recess."

"That's not fair! Just 'cause it's a little messy?"

"It's not a little messy, Caliph. It's a health hazard. The Department of Homeland Security would quarantine this school in a minute if they saw that." Then she pointed. "What's that green stuff in the corner?"

"Oh, wow! I've been looking for that! That's the piece of pizza I lost last month!"

"Why is it moving?!"

"Maybe it's hungry …" Caliph took a pair of scissors and stabbed at the piece of pizza, which picked up a broken pencil and fought back. The partridge watched silently.

"All right," said Mrs. Doopalapoozy turning to the rest of the class. "While Caliph tries to kill off his lunch, who would like to go next?"

No one raised his hand. The partridge flew out of the desk and landed on Mrs. Doopalapoozy's shoulder.

"AWK!" said the partridge.

"Quiet," said Mrs. Doopalapoozy. "I'm not in the mood."

## *The End*

The skin that I wear is the me people see,
But deep down inside is the realest me.
You can't see a heart by staring at skin;
What matters the most is the person within.

## LEARN FROM SCRIPTURE

This story is about more than clean desks and living pieces of pizza. What do you think the main point is? Does God just look at the outside of your life, or deep down into your heart? In 1 Samuel 16:7, God told Samuel "The LORD doesn't make decisions the way you do! People judge by outward appearance, but the LORD looks at a person's thoughts and intentions."

Let's ask God to clean out the junk in our hearts so we aren't ashamed to open ourselves up to him.

## END WITH PRAYER

God, the inside of my heart needs some cleaning. Dump out all the stuff that doesn't belong. Help me to be pure both inside and out. Amen.

# 22

# THE TWO SHEPHERDS

## FIND THIS OBJECT

A MAGNIFYING GLASS—Look through the magnifying glass at other people's faces. Have fun staring at each other's eyeballs or looking up each other's nostrils. Talk about what you would use a magnifying glass for or what you might search for with it.

If you don't have a magnifying glass, hide a favorite stuffed animal somewhere in the house. Then, turn off the lights and search with flashlights to see which of the children can find the lost animal first!

## ASK THESE QUESTIONS

Is there someone in this family who loses things all the time? What are some of the items that usually get lost? Have you ever lost something and then given up searching for it? Why did you give up? What determines how long and hard you'll keep searching for something?

## BEGIN THE STORY

Once upon a time there were two shepherds—one was named Gregory, and the other was named Nathan. One day a lamb wandered away from each of their flocks.

Gregory began to search for his lost sheep right away. He looked up in the mountains and down in caves and all through the meadows surrounding the hills. "Here, sheepy, sheepy, sheepy!" he called, but it was no use. No matter how hard he searched, he just couldn't find his sheep.

Nathan also began to search for his lost sheep. He also looked up in the mountains and down in the caves and all through the meadows surrounding the hills. "Here, sheepy, sheepy, sheepy!" he called, but it was no use. Nathan couldn't find his sheep, either.

When it began to get dark, Gregory decided to give up his search. "I'll never find my sheep!" he said. "I'm going home. C'mon, Nathan, let's go!"

"I think I'm going to keep looking," said Nathan.

"But it's getting dark," said Gregory.

"I know."

"It's dangerous out here."

"I know."

"There are wolves out here! And lions and tigers and—"

"I know, I know, bears. Oh, my!" said Nathan. "But my lamb is lost and scared and alone, and I want to find her."

"Well, I'm going home," said Gregory. "I'll see you later."

So Gregory went home and soon fell asleep. But Nathan kept searching—even when it became dark and dangerous—and the packs of hungry wolves and lions and tigers and bears roamed the mountains. Oh, my.

It was scary out there alone in the mountains, especially when the wild animals chased him and he almost stepped off the edge of a cliff. But Nathan didn't care about that nearly as much as he cared about finding his lost sheep.

It was just after midnight when he found his sheep! He put it on his shoulders and headed home to celebrate. The sheep was so happy to be found it wouldn't stop baaing and licking Nathan's neck. "All right! All right! That's enough!" he said with a laugh as his sheep slobbered all over his ears.

When he got home, Nathan was bruised and sore and scratched by thorns. He'd been chased by wolves and had almost fallen off a cliff, but he didn't care. He'd found his sheep, and that made it all worthwhile.

He found his friend Gregory fast asleep. Nathan set down his lamb and made sure she was safe. Then he headed back out into the night once again to search for Gregory's sheep. Because as long as any of the sheep were in danger, Nathan knew he wouldn't be able to sleep. After all, that's the kind of shepherd he was.

## *The End*

God is always searching for those who are lost,
He'll brave the danger and face the cost,
He'll search the mountains and the valleys deep,
Till he finds every lost and lonely sheep.

## LEARN FROM SCRIPTURE

Imagine being one of those lost sheep! Would you want a shepherd who would be willing to face the dark and dangerous hills to look for you, or one who would be just as happy to go back to bed and leave you to the wolves?

*(Be aware that some kids will say the wrong answer just to be silly. If they do, say, "Yeah, right! You'd be wolf chow!")*

Good shepherds risk everything, even their own lives, to save their sheep. Can you guess which shepherd in the story is more like Jesus?

*(Read and discuss the parable of the lost sheep in Luke 15:1–7.)*

Let's thank Jesus right now for loving us enough to search for us, even though it meant giving up his own life to save us.

## END WITH PRAYER

God, your grace means that you keep looking for us, even when our hearts have wandered far from you. Thanks for loving us and looking for us just like a good shepherd would. You're the best shepherd of all. Amen.

# 23

# THE FRIGHTENED DOVE

## FIND THIS OBJECT

A STUFFED BIRD OR A BIRD'S NEST—Talk about how fun it would be to fly. How high would you fly? Where would you go? Act like birds and fly around the kitchen, then gather together back at the nest (table) for the story.

## ASK THESE QUESTIONS

Sometimes people are afraid to try new things because they might fail, they might get embarrassed, or they might end up looking stupid. Why do you think people are often afraid to try new things? Have you ever been afraid to try something new because you thought you might fail at it? What did you do?

Listen to today's story poem and ask yourself what your nest is and what you might have to do to leave it.

## BEGIN THE STORY

Young bird in a nest; grew into a dove!
And mother urged with a gentle shove,
"You're free to fly and chase the breeze,
Take heart and leap and leave the trees!"

79

But the young dove feared and thought it best
To safely stay inside the nest.
*What if I fail? What if I fall?*
*What if I'm not meant to fly at all?*
*What if my wings are just too weak?*
*What if I hurt my neck or my beak?*
*What if I'm shot? Or killed? Or caught!*
*How can I fly? I've not been taught!*
*It's safer here. So, here I'll stay,*
*Perhaps I'll try some other day.*
Well, days turned to months and months turned to years.
And the dove never left the nest, or her fears.
She slowly grew old. And finally, she died.
She never fell, but she never *flew*,
For she never dared to try.[3]

## *The End*

## LEARN FROM SCRIPTURE

Why didn't the dove leave the nest? What do you think this story can teach us about life? When you hear the word *faith* what do you think of? Trusting in God and walking with God require a lot of faith.

Trusting in God means no longer clinging to what seems safe, but letting go of our safeguards and making God our only safety net. Isaiah wrote, "Those who wait on the LORD will find new strength. They will fly high on wings like eagles" (Isa. 40:31).

Let's ask God to give us the courage to trust him enough to let our faith soar to new heights.

## END WITH PRAYER

God, sometimes it's scary to try new things or to explore new shores. Give us the courage to dare, to step out in faith, and then live the full, rich life you have in mind for us. Help us to spread our wings and soar like eagles as we trust more and more in you. Amen.

# 24

# CLOUDS

## FIND THIS OBJECT

CRAWL AROUND ON THE FLOOR—Try to look at life from the perspective of a toddler or a baby.

## ASK THESE QUESTIONS

How do things look different from down here? How are they the same? Is it possible for two different people to see the same thing but understand it in completely different ways? Keep that in mind as I read today's story.

## BEGIN THE STORY

"Oh, look!" cried the child. "The clouds are on fire!"

"No, they're just reflecting the fire of the sun," said his mother. "Clouds have no fire of their own."

"Oh," said the child. And then he said, "Look! Now, the clouds are moving!"

"Well, yes, it looks as if they are," said the mother. "But perhaps it's only we who are moving, and the clouds are simply standing still."

"I see," said the child. And he watched the sky. "And now, the clouds are still!"

"Well, perhaps," said the mother. "Or maybe we are both moving very, very fast."

The child stared up at the clouds again. "And now, that cloud—there!—is turning into a unicorn!" said the child.

"It's only your mind that sees a unicorn in the clouds," said the mother. "Clouds don't turn into anything. It's all in your imagination."

"Oh," said the child. "I'd always thought clouds were more interesting than that."

And from then on, the child kept his eyes on the ground.

## *The End*

Two eyes to see the world. Two ears to hear its songs.
Some folks see all the blessings. Some folks see all the wrongs.
Some can hear the laughter of angels all around.
Do you stare at the stars above, or look down at the ground?

## LEARN FROM SCRIPTURE

What do you think this story can teach us?

*(Affirm their answers. If desired, just explore their responses. If you want to, read the following thoughts about seeing life through the eyes of a child.)*

Jesus appreciated and valued the innocence, faith, and humility of children. He never told children that they needed to become more like grown-ups, but he did tell grown-ups they needed to become more child-like. Children see the world in a special way adults can learn from. As Jesus said, "I assure you, unless you turn from your sins and become as little children, you will never get into the Kingdom of Heaven. Therefore, anyone who becomes as humble as this little child is the greatest in the Kingdom of Heaven" (Matt. 18:3–4).

Faith is sometimes hard for grown-ups because they find it harder to believe in the things they can't prove or don't see. Let's pray that God helps us to see the world through the eyes of a child, and that he helps us each find ways to remain childlike no matter how old we get.

# END WITH PRAYER

God, help us to see the world through your eyes—childlike, adventuresome, and full of wonder. You're cool and sometimes you do send unicorn-shaped clouds for all those who are willing to see them. Amen.

# 25

# FIGHTING THE TIGER

## FIND THIS OBJECT

PULL OUT A BUNCH OF PILLOWS and have a pillow fight as a family. (Remember to remove glasses and sharp objects from pockets first!) Then say, "Pillow fights can be lots of fun, but other kinds of fighting can leave people hurting or crying!"

## ASK THESE QUESTIONS

Have you ever had to deal with a bully at school?

What are some of the ways people usually deal with bullies?

Can you think of a good way to deal with a bully?

Today's story has an animal who is a bully. Let's see what happens when a couple of other animals get in his way.

## BEGIN THE STORY

Once upon a time, a jackal and a wolf were walking along a trail in the jungle when suddenly a large tiger appeared in front of them, blocking their way. "Get off my trail or I'll bite your tails off!" growled the tiger. He was big and strong and his voice was very gruff. "Now move!"

"It's not your trail!" said the jackal.

And the wolf added, "It's ours just as much as it is yours!"

"Well, I say it's mine—all mine!" said the tiger. "Go walk over there, through the thorns and quicksand!"

The wolf shook his head. "No thanks! I say you're just a big bully!"

"Me, too!" said the jackal. "C'mon! We can take him!"

When they said that, the tiger growled ferociously and rushed toward the wolf and the jackal. Even though there were two of them, the tiger easily beat them in the fight, scratching them with his sharp claws and biting their tails off just like he'd promised. As they limped away through the thorns and quicksand, the jackal said to the wolf, "I wish I were stronger so I could have beaten that tiger."

"I wish I were wiser," said the wolf, "so I wouldn't have gotten into that fight in the first place."

"Yeah, me, too." said the jackal. "'Cause now I'm gonna miss my tail."

"I know what you mean," said the wolf. "I know what you mean."

## The End

Sometimes the strongest thing you can do
Is be wiser than the one who is bullying you.

## LEARN FROM SCRIPTURE

Can you think of anything the jackal and the wolf might have done rather than argue with the bully? What would you have done?

The Bible reminds us that "Avoiding a fight is a mark of honor; only fools insist on quarreling" (Prov. 20:3). What are some good ways we can avoid fights and quarrels with others? Does it mean you're a fraidy cat if you don't want to get into a fight? Are there times when it might actually be all right to get into a fight?

The Bible says that only fools insist on quarreling and that we should live at peace with others as much as it depends on us (see Rom. 12:18). It also reminds us that "wisdom is better than strength" (Eccl. 9:16). Any time you can use wisdom to avoid a quarrel, it's probably the best thing to do—even if no one else notices. To close this devotion, I'd like to read you a poem that's based on a couple of Bible verses found in the book of Ecclesiastes:

There once was a wee little city;
Its walls were remarkably small.
Only a few people lived there;
There weren't many people at all.
A powerful king brought his army;
He completely surrounded the town.
He built sturdy ramps to attack it,
To climb up and over and down.
Now, there lived in the city a poor man
Who was wiser than all of the rest.
And through wisdom he saved the small city,
Though his fame was not what you'd guess—
Because no one remembered that poor man
Who had shown just how wise that he was
And in time, that man was forgotten,
And I'll tell you, I think it's because,
When help is no longer needed,
And we can walk safely ahead
Then wisdom is no longer heeded
And we despise what the wise ones have said.[4]

It sure would be cool to know how that wise man saved his city! Too bad the Bible doesn't tell us how he did it. Even if we don't know *how* he did it, we can probably guess *why* he did it—because avoiding a fight is a mark of honor. Let's try to do the same thing: Use wisdom to avoid quarrels with others.

## END WITH PRAYER

God, I want to be wise, but it's not always easy. Teach me to seek peace, avoid quarrels, and become wiser—whether other people notice or not. Amen.

# 26

# THE PRINCE'S WISHES

## FIND THIS OBJECT

A LAMP—Explain that long ago many people believed genies lived in lamps and, according to legend, kind genies could grant people wishes!

## ASK THESE QUESTIONS

Have you ever heard the story about Aladdin's Lamp? It's a very old story about a boy who finds a magic lamp with a genie inside and gets three wishes. If you could wish for anything in the whole wide world, what would you wish for?

*(Allow them to respond and share what you yourself might wish for.)*

Listen carefully to this story. It's about a prince who in the end probably wished he hadn't wished for what he wished for.

## BEGIN THE STORY

*(As you read this story, try to give the genie and the prince different voices. Make the prince's character whiny and annoying and make the genie a hip-hop rapper with a bad attitude. Have fun!)*

Once upon a time there was prince who was very greedy and not very happy. He always wanted more, more, more! One day as he was walking through the forest he saw a glint of something shiny beneath a pile of leaves next to a baby oak tree. When he pushed the leaves aside, he discovered a genie lamp! He rubbed it … rubbed it … rubbed it … and—*zap-flowie!*—out came a powerful genie.

"Whoa," said the prince.

"Zap-flowie," said the genie. "What's up? I'll grant you three wishes, dude!"

"Three? Only three?"

"Yeah, three. Ya got a problem wi' dat?"

"Um … well …"

"And don't be askin' me to make you younger or make you live forever—stuff like that. Homey don't go there."

"Who cares about all that!" said the prince. "I want more wishes! I want a *million* more wishes!"

"Yo, whatever. Your wish is my command and all that stuff, that sweet funky stuff. Zap-flowie! All right, there you go. You got a million more wishes. You had three, you used one, so that's two—plus the one million you wished for. Now you got a million and two wishes."

"Well, I want another millio—no wait! I want a *billion* more wishes!"

"Zap-flowie," said the genie. "You got a billion more. You now have one billion, one million and one wishes left."

"All right! Then I wish for two billion more wishes!" said the prince.

"Zap-flowie," said the genie.

And so it went. Wish after wish after wish. Until the prince was no longer a little boy, but an old man. And he wasn't sitting next to a baby tree anymore, but a great spreading oak, and the genie was saying, "Zap-flowie. You now have six hundred ninety-one trillion, five hundred fifty-seven billion, four hundred twenty-two million, nine hundred eleven thousand and four wishes."

And then, just as the prince was about to wish for a gazillion more wishes, a lightning bolt struck the tree and it fell on top of him and squished him pretty much as flat as a pancake. And he never got to use any of those six hundred ninety-one trillion, five hundred fifty-seven billion, four hundred twenty-two million, nine hundred eleven thousand and four wishes.

And the genie just shook his head. "Yo, when will they ever learn?" he said. And then he went back into his lamp and waited patiently for the next greedy person to come along.

## The End

When you're greedy, all you think of is getting more stuff.
But the richest people know they already have enough.

# LEARN FROM SCRIPTURE

Think about these words that Solomon wrote nearly three thousand years
ago: "Those who love money will never have enough. How absurd to think
that wealth brings true happiness! The more you have, the more people
come to help you spend it. So what is the advantage of wealth—except perhaps to watch it run through your fingers! ... People who live only for
wealth come to the end of their lives as naked and empty-handed as on the
day they were born" (Eccl. 5:10–11, 15).

What do you think of that?

In Colossians 3:5 Paul writes that greed is idolatry. *(You may need to
explain to younger children that idolatry is letting something other than God
fill our hearts.)* When we're greedy and thinking only of ourselves, we show
that things are more important to us than God is. Wishing for more and
more all the time shows we're not content with what we have. Jesus warned
people over and over to be content and to pursue his kingdom above
earthly stuff. He even told a story about it.

*(Read or retell Jesus' parable of the foolish rich man in Luke 12:16–20.)*

What's even more important than storing up earthly wealth? What
might be a good prayer for us to pray today?

# END WITH PRAYER

God, we're sorry for all the times we've been greedy and grabby.
Fill our hearts and our lives with your love instead. Our biggest
wish of all is that the things you want to happen would be done
in our lives. Amen.

# 27

# THE RIVER

## FIND THIS OBJECT

ONE OR MORE STUFFED ANIMALS (preferably ones that might play near a river or lake)—Make the animals talk to each other and tell each other about their homes.

## ASK THESE QUESTIONS

Compare where the animals live to where you live. What similarities are there? What differences?

Some people move all over the place, from one house to another, one family to another, or from one state or country to another. Do you know any people like that? What are some of the reasons people move around so much? Think about that as I read today's story.

## BEGIN THE STORY

Once there was a beautifully clear river that rushed down from the mountains and emptied into a green valley. The river was happy and reflected the sunlight up to the sky like a thousand diamonds.

One day, a group of travelers approached the shore of the great river. They'd come from a distant desert and had been traveling many weeks. They were hot and tired, and the river was a welcome sight.

Oh, they'd never seen such a beautiful river! They watched the sun shimmering on the water. They splashed along the shore. They played in the shallow wave pools and drank the crystal clear water. The people fell in love with the river and the animals that lived along its banks.

"Being near this river is much better than being in the desert!" they said. "There's room to play and swim. There's fresh water to drink. Let's stay here by the river! Let's live here!" And so the people decided to settle by the shore of the mighty river.

They found the remains of a deserted town there and began to repair the buildings. Soon, all the travelers had moved into homes beside the river. They planted crops in the nearby valleys. At sunset, they washed and swam in the golden waters. They were thankful to have such a wonderful place for their home.

And the people were happy—at least for a while.

But then, little by little, they stopped swimming in the river as much as they had at first. Less and less did they notice the sun shimmering off the water. Fewer and fewer people splashed along the shore of the river. They became busier and busier, making their homes larger and developing new ways of using the river's power to warm their homes and water their fields. When the crops were slow to grow, the people began to hunt the river animals.

Many people forgot why they'd stopped to live by the river in the first place. Some forgot the truth about how harsh the desert was and began to miss living there.

Then one day, a man came walking down a trail from one of the mountains on the horizon. He had beautiful rocks in his pocket from the stream high in the peaks where the river was born. He told the people about white crystals that fell from the sky up in the mountains and turned to water in your hands. He said that the weather in the mountains was cool, not hot like that of the desert, and that the view from the mountains was much prettier than it was down here in the valley. He invited the people to join him on his return trip to the mountains, and the more they listened to the man's stories, the more the people began to stare longingly at the faraway mountains.

One by one they packed up their belongings, and everyone in the town followed the man toward the mountain range. They left their fields. They left their homes. They didn't even turn back to say goodbye to the river. Finally, the only thing that was left to show they'd lived there at all was the remains of a deserted town.

As the river watched the people leave its shores and climb up the side of the mountain, it remembered a time long ago, before the desert people, before the ruined town. One sunny day it had heard strange noises—shouts from a group of people coming down from the mountains. They'd stopped by the shore of the river and built a small town. They'd played in the river and watched the sun shimmer on the water. But one day, they'd grown tired of the river and set off on a journey far away, toward a desert.

Rivers remember things like that.

And as it did, it wondered if those lonely pilgrims would ever be as happy as the splashing animals that never moved away from its banks.

## The End

We soon get used to the things that we see.
What's new? What's different? What's on TV?
When we hope something new will make us happy somehow,
We miss all the beauty of the here and the now.

## LEARN FROM SCRIPTURE

Long ago a Christian writer named Augustine wrote a short prayer to God that went like this: "My soul was restless until it learned to rest in you." What do you think he meant? Our souls are the parts of our hearts that make us each special and different. Why are our souls so restless? What do you think people are really looking for when they move so much from one job or place to another?

Who do you think the man from the mountains might represent?

As long as we believe happiness is out there somewhere, wrapped up in a different place—a new toy, a new teacher, or the latest video game— we'll be missing out on the gifts this moment has to offer. Right here, right now, God's rest and peace are available to all who will let him step in. Maybe that's why the river animals were so happy. They discovered what so many of us are still looking for.

Solomon put it this way, "Enjoy what you have rather than desiring what you don't have. Just dreaming about nice things is meaningless; it is like chasing the wind" (Eccl. 6:9).

## END WITH PRAYER

God, help us to find our rest in you, and our peace in your love. When the world lets us down, remind us that you are here— right now, right here—wherever that might be. Amen.

# 28

# COLORING OUTSIDE THE LIONS

## FIND THIS OBJECT

A COLORING BOOK——If desired, let the kids color while you read the story.

## ASK THESE QUESTIONS

Do you think it's important to color inside the lines?

Is there a right way to color a picture? Explain what you mean.

When you're painting or coloring, is it okay to make things whatever color you want? Why or why not?

## BEGIN THE STORY

Once there was an empty coloring book named Brianna who sat on the shelf at the store feeling rather bland and sad—and of course, very empty. She wished more than anything else that she were colorful like the picture books just across the aisle. From where she sat, they looked absolutely perfect!

While she was thinking those thoughts, a girl chewing strawberry bubble gum picked her up.

"Mommy! Mommy!" cried the girl, whose name was Suzy. "Can we buy it? Huh? Huh? Can we? Please, Mommy? Pretty please ... with sugar on top?"

"Oh, I suppose," sighed her mother, who had already said no three hundred and eleven times that afternoon and was just glad that Suzy hadn't picked up another doll.

"And this!" said Suzy, picking up another doll.

"No," said her mother as she hurried to the checkout counter. "Just the coloring book."

And so they bought Brianna and drove home.

*Oh, I hope she's a good colorer!* Brianna thought as Suzy carried her into the living room and pulled out her crayons. *I hope she colors inside the lines so I'm as pretty as a picture book. I hate being so empty! I want to be beautiful!*

But as everyone knows, girls who chew strawberry bubble gum do not like to color inside the lines. And soon Suzy had scribbled all over the first five pages of the book. She had created a purple sky and an orange fish and a giant pink hippo. She'd also colored a whole page of lions green with blue polka dots.

*Oh, no!* Brianna thought. *I don't look like the real world at all! I'm ruined!*

But when Suzy's mother saw the picture she smiled and said, "How lovely! You've colored the world in a whole new way!" And Suzy blew a big strawberry-flavored bubble to show that she was happy about it too.

Her mother reached down to rip out the sheet with the green lions. Oh, Brianna was frightened! She thought it would hurt terribly to be torn apart! But in a moment it was all over, and it hadn't hurt a bit because of those itty bitty holes down the side of the page. *So that's what those holes are for,* she thought. *Hee, hee, hee! That tickles!*

Suzy's mother put the picture of the green lions on the refrigerator for everyone to see. Then she smiled and Suzy smiled, and even the lions seemed to smile.

And from then on Brianna watched as her pages were hung on the refrigerator, one after another. She realized the pages from the picture books never appeared on the fridge. *Only my pages are special enough to get put up there!* she thought. And every day, even though she had fewer and fewer pages, Brianna felt less and less empty inside.

## *The End*

When we're busy comparing to try and feel good,
We'll never be happy or feel like we should.
The gifts that God gives to your life and mine,
Are different on purpose, by his plan and design.

## LEARN FROM SCRIPTURE

It's easy to feel empty and useless when we compare ourselves to others. Does God want us to compare ourselves to others? Why do you say that? Sometimes comparing ourselves helps us feel better about ourselves, and sometimes it makes us feel worse, but either way we usually feel that way for the wrong reason.

Each one of us is unique, and God wants to send his Spirit down to turn us each into great works of art: "For we are God's masterpiece. He has created us anew in Christ Jesus, so that we can do the good things he planned for us long ago" (Eph. 2:10).

Long ago God planned good things for us to do. We are each unique and the ways we serve him will often look quite different. Let's pray that he'll help us to notice and appreciate the unique gifts we each have so we can stop trying to be like other people.

## END WITH PRAYER

Dear God, color my life however you like! Without you I'm empty inside. I may not look like other people, but that's okay. You made me like this for a special reason. I'm ready for you to fill me and let the world see the artwork of your love shining through my life. Amen.

# 29

# MURRAY THE EEL

## FIND THIS OBJECT

A CANDY BAR or another tasty treat that everyone in your family likes—Discuss what makes it so tempting and whether or not it's easy to say no when it's offered.

## ASK THESE QUESTIONS

What is something you have trouble saying no to? What makes it so hard to say no to it? Most of us have areas of our lives in which it's difficult to be self-controlled. As I read today's story, think about your life and the things you might have trouble with, just like Murray does.

## BEGIN THE STORY

Murray the Eel lived in a cave with a very narrow opening. The cave entrance was just big enough for a normal-sized eel to fit through. But that was the problem. You see, Murray was not a normal-sized eel. He was a large eel. He was an overweight eel. Actually, Murray was a great big, fat, lazy eel.

And every day Murray would sit by the opening to his cave and wait for food to float by. He didn't go outside his cave because he couldn't fit

97

through the cave entrance. Instead, he just lay there in the dark, and when food floated by he would gobble it up.

Yum. Yum. Yum.

Now I should mention that even though he hadn't left the cave in years, Murray wanted very badly to see the rest of the ocean. He really did. But to do that, he would have to lose weight. "Someday," he'd say to himself as he waited for more food to float by. "Someday I'll lose weight and go exploring! Someday I'll leave this cave and swim all the way to the other side of the ocean!"

But then a nice, juicy piece of eel food would float by. And he would gobble it up. Yum! Yum! Yum! And then he'd say, "Tomorrow! That's it! Tomorrow I'll start my diet! That's what I'll do!"

But you already know what happened. The next day Murray would do the same thing, and the day after that the same thing again. So, of course, the someday he'd been waiting for never came, and Murray the Eel lived the rest of his life in that cave dreaming about the far side of the ocean.[5]

## The End

Saying no when we need to, and yes when we should,
Will lead us toward freedom and the things that are good.

## LEARN FROM SCRIPTURE

Just like Murray, we sometimes stay trapped by our inability to be self-controlled. We put things off for too long, and then one day it's too late to make the choice we'd like to make.

Learning when to say no to something is as important as learning when to say yes to something. Yet even self-control comes by the grace of God. As it says in the Bible, "For the grace of God that brings salvation has appeared to all men. It teaches us to say 'No' to ungodliness and worldly passions, and to live self-controlled, upright and godly lives in this present age" (Titus 2:11–12 NIV).

God's grace helps us choose what is right and helps us live the self-controlled lives he has in mind for us. Learning when to say yes and when to say no is something God will help us do if we let him. Let's ask for the courage to make the decisions we need to make right now.

# END WITH PRAYER

God, forgive me for the times I've blown it. I don't want my bad choices to trap me. Show me when to say yes and when to say no. And when I have a hard time doing it, use your grace to make up for my weakness. Thanks, God. Amen.

# 30

# CLAY POTS

## FIND THIS OBJECT

A CLAY FLOWER POT OR VASE—Talk about the pot's purpose. Why is it the size or shape that it is? Is it fulfilling its purpose now? Why or why not?

## ASK THESE QUESTIONS

When a potter makes a pot, do you think he does so with the purpose of the pot in mind? Why do you say that? If you were making a pot to hold a Christmas tree, how would you make it? What about a lily? What if it were going to hold a life-sized statue of a dragon? A golden treasure?

Our story today is about a potter who makes pots with a very unusual purpose, indeed.

## BEGIN THE STORY

Derek wanted to buy a clay pot, so he went to a pottery store and began to look over all the pots that were on the shelves.

There were pots, pots, pots galore!
Five pots, ten pots, many pots more!

There were pots all over the store.
Some were wide, some were narrow, some small.
Some were short, some were stubby, some tall.
Some pots were dainty and others were thick;
Still others had covers that liked to stick.
Piled up to the ceiling and stacked on the floor,
There were pots all over the store!

The potter sat on a small stool beside his pottery wheel, carefully shaping a pot with his hands. He pumped the pottery wheel with his foot and slapped fresh, wet clay onto the pot he was forming. He also reached into his pocket and dropped something into the pot. And, as the wheel spun around, the potter moved his fingers up and down, saying:

Pots, pots, pots galore!
Five pots, ten pots, many pots more!
Pots all over the store!
Some are wide, some are narrow, some small.
Some are short, some are stubby, some tall.
Some pots are dainty and others are thick;
Still others have covers that like to stick.
Piled up to the ceiling and stacked on the floor,
There are pots all over the store!
Yeah!

As Derek looked over the pots, he began to notice something—each of the pots had a crack in it. Some cracks were only visible upon close inspection. Others were large and long and easy to see. Derek couldn't find a single perfect pot in the whole store.

"These pieces of pottery are worthless!" he said to the potter. "Every one of them has a crack in it!"

The potter stopped spinning the wheel and looked up at Derek. "Each one is specially designed by me. How can you call them worthless?"

"But none of them are perfect! They all have flaws!"

"Maybe I put the cracks in there on purpose," the potter said.

"Humph," said Derek. "What purpose could a crack serve?"

The potter went back to his work. "You'd be surprised what the cracks can reveal," he said. "So, young man, would you like to buy a pot or not?"

Derek sighed. "Yeah, I guess so. I'll take this one." He chose the pot with the smallest crack in it. That way, he figured no one would notice it. Then, he paid for the pot, brought it home, and stuck it on the shelf in his bedroom.

And because he'd chosen a pot with such a small crack in it, he never noticed the gold coins glistening inside.

> Piled up to the ceiling and stacked on the floor,
> There are pots all over the store!

## The End

> The Potter has a purpose for every pot he shapes;
> The Potter puts a treasure in every pot he makes.
> Few people may notice or realize,
> But look through the cracks and you'll notice the prize.

## LEARN FROM SCRIPTURE

What kind of potter would put gold into a pot he was going to get rid of? Can you think of any important truths this story can teach us?

Long ago Isaiah wrote, "LORD, you are our Father. We are the clay, and you are the potter. We are all formed by your hand" (Isa. 64:8).

God is the potter, the shaper of lives. He makes each of us special and unique. In addition, God's Word is a precious treasure that all Christians carry around in their hearts. As the Bible says, "We have this treasure in jars of clay to show that this all-surpassing power is from God and not from us" (2 Cor. 4:7 NIV). Christians carry a treasure inside them and often it's only through the cracks in our lives that people will notice the treasure inside of our hearts.

## END WITH PRAYER

> God, we ask that you would put your word deep into our hearts. Help other people to see your love in our lives. Remind us that you shaped us as you did for a reason. You are the Potter, we are the clay. Shape us and use us as you wish. Amen.

# 31

# SIEGFRIED THE SQUIRREL

## FIND THIS OBJECT

A MEDAL OR A TROPHY—Talk about trying to win first place in a competition. Is it possible to be good at something and not show off? Why is it so easy to start showing off?

## ASK THESE QUESTIONS

Have you ever seen anyone who is a show-off or who likes to brag? How do they make you feel—happier or more annoyed? Do you respect people more or less when you see them show off?

Let's see what happens to the show-off in this story.

## BEGIN THE STORY

Siegfried the Squirrel loved to show off by running back and forth across the road. "Watch how close I can get to the cars!" he yelled.

"No, Siegfried!" warned his mother. "Stay off the road! You remember what happened to your Uncle Wilhelm! He almost got flattened by a pickup truck!"

"Oh, I'll be all right!" said Siegfried and he ran out into the road. A great big truck was coming down the highway at seventy-five miles per hour.

"Oh, goody!" said Siegfried. "Watch this!"

He dashed out of the way just as the truck zoomed past.

*Varoom!*

"See!" said Siegfried, "Nothing to worry abou—"

And just then a motorcycle Siegfried had not seen turned the corner and ran right over his tail.

"Ouch!" he cried and ran into the forest.

"Oh, Siegfried!" said his mother. "I warned you! Are you okay?"

"I think so," said Siegfried, rubbing his tail, which was now quite flat and had tread marks across the top of it. And he couldn't run nearly so fast anymore, dragging that big flat tail behind him. And from then on, the other squirrels told him he looked more like a beaver than a squirrel.

## The End

Those who show off may look cool at first,
But the place they'll end up in is the one that's the worst.

## LEARN FROM SCRIPTURE

Jesus had a lot to say about humility and showing off. One time he told the people who liked to show off, "The proud will be humbled, but the humble will be honored" (Luke 14:11). Pride never leads to anything good (see Prov. 16:18). Rather than trying to prove how great we are or how much honor we deserve, we should spend our lives in trying to prove how great God is and how much honor he deserves.

## END WITH PRAYER

God, teach us humility and keep us from the temptation to show off. Rather than trying to get the praise of people, help us to live for your applause instead. Make us humble enough to listen to your word, and bold enough to obey it. Amen.

# 32

# THE MOON GIFT

## FIND THIS OBJECT

A TELESCOPE—Or make a fake one out of a paper towel roll. Take turns looking through it at each other or around the neighborhood. If you're reading this story at nighttime, go outside and look up at the moon, stars, or sky.

## ASK THESE QUESTIONS

Do you know what an astronomer does? He studies the stars and the sky. Can you think of something that would be cool about a job like that? If you could name a brand new star, what would you name it?

Everyone can learn from the stars, even if you don't have a telescope. Today's story is about one of the lessons that the stars, moon, and sky can teach us.

## BEGIN THE STORY

Once there was a prince named Tishwan Bookie. Everyone thought his dad was the richest man in the world. Everyone thought King Bookie was the most powerful king there was.

Each year Prince Bookie got anything he wanted for Christmas. And every year, one week before Christmas, he would go up to his dad and say, "Dad, Dad! I want more stuff! Gimme! Gimme! Gimme! Gimme! Gimme more stuff!" And his dad would get it for him.

But when the prince turned twelve, his dad said, "Tishwan, I've gotten you everything there is to get! You have your own castle, a pet dragon, five hundred horses, and your own brand of octopus-flavored bubble gum that's more popular in some villages than potato soup! What more could you possibly want?"

Tishwan had to think about that. After all, he did own almost everything there was to own. Finally he said, "This year for Christmas, I want the moon!"

"The moon! How am I supposed to get you the moon? Who will I buy it from?"

"Figure it out, Dad," he said. "You have one week! Gimme! Gimme! Gimme! Gimme! Gimme more stuff!"

Well, all that happened on Monday morning, and all day long King Bookie did everything he could do to try to buy the moon. He talked to other kings and emperors, he called in wise men and clever women, and he asked them all, "Do you know, do you know who owns the moon? Do you know who owns the moon up above?" But no one knew who owned the moon, so no one could sell it to him.

The next day, Queen Bookie said to her husband, "Dear, whoever owns the moon must also own the sun. Find out who owns the sun and you'll know who owns the moon. It only makes sense."

So King Bookie asked everyone, "Do you know, do you know who owns the sun? Do you know who owns the sun and the moon up above?" But no one knew who owned the sun, so no one could sell him the moon.

On Wednesday morning, Queen Bookie said, "Dear, whoever owns the sun must also own the stars."

"Yes, yes, you're right!" he said. "The stars!" And that day, King Bookie asked everyone, "Do you know, do you know who owns the stars? Do you know who owns the stars and the sun and the moon up above?" But no one knew who owned the stars, so no one could sell him the moon.

On Thursday, Queen Bookie said, "Dear, whoever owns the stars must also own the sky."

"The sky! Yes, of course, the sky!" So King Bookie asked everyone, "Do you know, do you know who owns the sky? Do you know who owns the sky and the stars and the sun and the moon up above?" But no one knew who owned the sky, so no one could sell him the moon.

On Friday, Queen Bookie said, "Dear, whoever owns the sky must also own the wind."

"The wind, you say? All right then." And King Bookie asked everyone, "Do you know, do you know who owns the wind? Do you know who owns the wind and the sky, and the stars and the sun, and the moon up above?" But no one knew who owned the wind, so no one could sell him the moon.

On Saturday morning, Queen Bookie said, "I have one last idea, dear. Whoever owns the wind must also own the waves on the ocean and the ripples on the sea."

"Waves and ripples," sighed King Bookie. "All right, here I go." And he asked everyone, "Do you know, do you know who owns the waves? Do you know who owns the waves and the wind, and the sky, and the stars and the sun and the moon up above?" But no one knew who owned the waves on the ocean or the ripples on the sea, so no one could sell him the moon.

Finally, on Sunday afternoon, with only one day left, King Bookie went for a long walk along the beach. He watched the sun set above the ocean and the stars slowly come out. He looked up at the moon shining in the sky, and he felt the waves tickle across his feet as the wind whispered past his ears. He thought, *If I don't own the moon or the sun or the stars or the sky or the wind or even the waves, then I'm certainly not the greatest king of all; and I'm not the richest man in the world, either. Whoever is in charge of these is far, far richer than I!*

Then King Bookie thought about how the sun and the moon and the stars always went where they were told to and did as they were supposed to, and how the sky never went on vacation, and the wind could be counted on to carry seeds around the land, and the tides kept their daily appointments with the shore. *How obedient are his subjects!* thought the king. *Whoever rules the sky and the stars and the wind and the waves must be a much greater king than I, as well!*

The next day, on Christmas Eve, when Tishwan Bookie returned to his dad for the moon gift saying, "Gimme! Gimme! Gimme! Gimme! Gimme more stuff!" King Bookie took him for a walk along the beach and told him about the King that was greater than he was. He told the prince about the one who rules the wind and the waves, the sky and the stars, the sun and the moon, and the ripples on the sea.

And even if Tishwan was too young to realize it yet, that gift was even greater than the moon in the sky up above.

## The End

> The world all around us, the moon in the sky,
> The sun and the waves and the wind whistling by,
> All speak of their maker and tell of his might,
> The sun in the day and the stars through the night.

## LEARN FROM SCRIPTURE

Did you know that there's a storyteller who's talking all the time, but most people don't hear the stories? This storyteller speaks in a language you can't hear with your ears, but that all honest people can hear with their hearts. Do you have any idea what storyteller I'm talking about?

Listen to these words from Psalm 19:1–4: "The heavens tell of the glory of God. The skies display his marvelous craftsmanship. Day after day they continue to speak; night after night they make him known. They speak without a sound or a word; their voice is silent in the skies; yet their message has gone out to all the earth, and their words to all the world."

Every day and every night the sky and the rest of God's creation tell us about his glory, his everlasting nature, and his great power. It's humbling to think that such a great and powerful king loves us enough to call us his children. But he does. And he gave us the greatest Christmas gift of all—himself.

## END WITH PRAYER

> God, you are the greatest king of all! Everything in all of creation is an arrow pointing to how mighty you are and how great you are. Remind us of your greatness every time we feel the wind in our face, watch the sun set, or see the stars or moon shining in the night. Amen.

# 33

# PRINCESS ALAMORE

## FIND THIS OBJECT

A SCHOOL YEARBOOK OR CLASS PICTURE—Talk about the different people you admire, point out the ones who are your friends, and the ones you would like to get to know better.

## ASK THESE QUESTIONS

What are some good ways to become better friends with someone? Which of those ways will help us become better friends with Jesus? Today's story teaches us a lot about friendship with Jesus and how to become more like him.

## BEGIN THE STORY

Once upon a time in a faraway land, there was a beautiful princess named Princess Alamore. She rode her horse more skillfully, shot a bow and arrow more accurately, and danced more gracefully than anyone else in the kingdom.

Of course, all the other girls wanted to be like Princess Alamore. They wished they could ride like her, shoot like her, and dance like her. And, of course, all of them wished they were as beautiful as the princess.

So they watched from a distance and made notes on how she sat upon her horse and held the reigns and moved with the horse's movements. And they tried to imitate her, but when they did, they fell off the horse and into the mud. Ouch.

Then they bought the same type of bow and used the same type of arrows as Princess Alamore. But when they tried to shoot like her, they missed the target and hit people right in their rear ends! Yow!

And when they danced, they pretended to be Princess Alamore, but they stepped on the toes of their partners so much that the young men had to duct tape pillows to their feet just so they wouldn't leave the dance floor all black and blue and with bruised toes.

One day an orphan girl named Amy said, "I want to be just like Princess Alamore when I grow up!" But her friends laughed at her. "You'll never be like the princess," they said. "She's beautiful and graceful, and you're ugly and clumsy!"

Their words made Amy sad but determined. So one day as Princess Alamore was riding through her orchard, Amy went out to meet her. She bowed low and said, "Your majesty, I would like to learn to ride like you, but I don't know how, and there's no one to teach me."

"Oh, Amy! You don't know how long I've been waiting for one of the girls in the kingdom to ask me that!"

"You know my name?"

"Of course. I know the names of all the children in my kingdom. Here, climb up and let me teach you what I know."

And so Princess Alamore taught Amy to ride straight and true and to balance upon the horse's back. And she taught her how to shoot and to look past the arrow to the target and let the bowstring glide off her fingers. And she showed her how you can disappear into the music when you dance by letting the music disappear into you.

But the more time Amy spent with the princess, the more the other girls made fun of her. "You think you're better than everyone else now just because you're with the princess all the time!" they said.

"No, it's not like that," said Amy. "She would spend time with you, too, if only you'd let her!"

But the other girls just scoffed and walked away.

One day, Princess Alamore came up to Amy. "I'm going to visit my father at the other end of the kingdom," she said. "While I'm gone I want you to remember everything I taught you."

"Okay, I will," said Amy. "I promise."

Then Princess Alamore left. And for a while Amy did just as she'd promised. For a while she remembered to dance and shoot and ride just like Princess Alamore. But then, in time, she began to go back to her old habits and her old friends. She began to shoot and miss the target and hit people in their rear ends. Ouch!

And she began to fall off her horse again, down into the mud. Yuck!

And she began to step on the toes of her dance partners just like her old friends did while they danced. Out came the pillows and duct tape.

One day, a neighboring ruler named Lord Darken heard that Princess Alamore had left to visit her father the king. *Aha, now that she's gone this is my chance!* he thought. *With a hundred of my horsemen I'll take over her part of the kingdom!*

So he gathered one hundred of his strongest swordsmen and one hundred of his fastest steeds and rode toward Princess Alamore's part of the kingdom. When Amy heard he was coming she thought, *WWPAD?—What would Princess Alamore do? She would stop him, I know she would!*

So Amy ran out to the field with her bow and arrow as Lord Darken approached. And she followed the strides of Lord Darken's horse and let the arrow fly straight and true, not at him, but at the horse's reigns. The arrow cut the reigns and Lord Darken said, "Uh-oh!" and fell face first into the mud.

He leaped to his feet and drew his sword. "I'll run you through!"

"Oh, no you won't!" said Amy, gracefully dancing out of the way as Lord Darken lunged at her and missed and landed once again in the mud. Some of it even went up his nose. Yuck.

Amy climbed onto his horse.

"You'll never be able to ride that horse!" yelled the muddy Lord Darken.

"Oh, yes I will!" said Amy. She remembered all that the princess had shown her. She rode to the far side of the kingdom and told Princess Alamore and her father, the king, about Lord Darken. The king brought his knights and captured Lord Darken and all of his swordsmen and threw them into the dungeon. Then, Princess Alamore went to talk to Amy.

"While I was gone, did you remember what I told you?"

"At first I did," said Amy. Then she shook her head sadly. "But then I forgot and went back to my old friends. I'm so sorry." Amy thought for sure the princess would be angry at her.

But Princess Alamore didn't yell or scold or accuse. "I forgive you, Amy," she said. "And I wanted to tell you, my father has invited you to live with us at the palace. He wants to adopt you, Amy. He wants you to be his very own daughter."

"But I don't deserve it, I—"

"Of course you don't deserve it," said Princess Alamore rather sternly. "He's a king! No one deserves it. But he's *chosen* you, Amy. He loves you and I do too, and we want you to join our family. Do you understand?"

Amy nodded.

"Do you accept his invitation?"

There were tears in Amy's eyes as she nodded her head. "Oh, yes! Oh, most certainly, yes!"

And so Amy became a child of the king. She moved into the palace and spent all of her time with Princess Alamore.

And from then on, when princes would visit from faraway lands, some would ask to dance with Princess Alamore, and some would ask to dance with her sister, Amy. For they'd become so much alike, it was hard to tell the two of them apart.[6]

## *The End*

There's a reason to celebrate, a reason to sing!
For all who believe are now children of the king!

## LEARN FROM SCRIPTURE

When Amy went to spend time with the princess, how did her friends treat her? Why do you think she went back to her old habits while Princess Alamore was gone? What can we learn from this story to help us be better friends with Jesus?

The good news is that Jesus wants to be more than just friends with us, he actually wants us to become his brothers and sisters as we are adopted into the family of his Father, the King. As John wrote, "But to all who believed him and accepted him, he gave the right to become children of God" (John 1:12); "See how very much our heavenly Father loves us, for he allows us to be called his children" (1 John 3:1).

*(This story gives a good opportunity for explaining the gospel to your family. If they have never done so, invite your children to trust in Christ as their Savior.)*

## END WITH PRAYER

Jesus, we want to be with you and become more like you—not from a distance, but close up, as a part of your family. We love you only because you loved us first. Amen.

## 34

# THE WEIGHT-LIFTING FROG

## FIND THIS OBJECT

A BUNCH OF TOOLS, such as a hammer, pliers, and a wrench

## ASK THESE QUESTIONS

*(Explain to the children that you're going to show them how to use the tools. But then, when you begin, use the wrong tool for the wrong job! For example, try to unscrew a bolt with the hammer, or pull out a nail with the pliers. Have fun with it. Be goofy. "Hmm, why won't this work? Oh, so you think this is the wrong tool? Which one is the right tool?" Try the wrong one again.)*

Tools are designed for a specific purpose. All of us are made to worship God, just like all tools are made to build or fix stuff. Yet each tool is made to do a different job, and we're each made different and special by God. Should the hammer feel bad because it's not a wrench? Or the pliers feel bad it's not a screwdriver? Sometimes we can get confused when we don't match up our gifts with what God has given us to do, something Frog is about to find out the hard way.

# BEGIN THE STORY

Once there was a frog who wanted to be a weight lifter. "Stick to being a great hopper," his friends told him. "You're good at that! After all, you were made to hop!"

But the frog didn't listen to them. "Forget hopping," he said. "I want a great-looking chest and awesome abs! I wanna be pumped!" So, instead of practicing hopping, he lifted weights every day until his arms were huge. He had muscles bulging out all over.

"You look silly," his friends told him.

"I look awesome," he said. "I can bench-press a tree!" And then, just to prove it, he did.

An alligator who lived on the other side of the pond saw the tree moving up and down and wondered what was going on. He swam over and saw the muscular frog set down the tree.

"You are very strong, indeed," said the alligator, edging closer to the bank.

"Yup," said Frog, somewhat breathlessly—after all, he was in the middle of a very difficult workout. "I think I might be voted Mr. Amphibian next year!"

"But how well can you hop?" asked Alligator.

"Who cares about hopping?" said Frog. "I can bench-press a tree!"

"So you can't hop at all?"

"Not any more," said Frog, flexing his muscles. "But check out these biceps!"

"Oh, good," said Alligator. "I was hoping you'd say that." And then, with a swish of his mighty tail, he swam closer to Frog, and opened up his mouth. When Frog saw Alligator's teeth, he tried to hop away, but, of course, his arm muscles were so big and heavy they weighed him down. And his leg muscles were so wimpy that he couldn't hop too well. He just tipped over instead and landed on his face.

And that day the alligator ate up the foolish frog, and some of the animals heard him say, as he finished licking his chops, "That's the tastiest Mr. Amphibian I've ever had."

## The End

A fool only does what he wants to do,
But wise people are thoughtful about what they pursue.

## LEARN FROM SCRIPTURE

Have you heard of Samson before? What made Samson special? What was his gift? Samson was gifted by God to be a great warrior, but most of the time he did what *he* wanted rather than what *God* wanted him to do with his life. Like the frog in our story, Samson was made for one thing, but he pursued another, until in the end it destroyed him.

In another part of the Bible, Paul says, "All of you together are Christ's body, and each one of you is a separate and necessary part of it" (1 Cor. 12:27). Part of being faithful to God is discovering what he has gifted us each to do, and then using those gifts to serve God and share his love with others.

## END WITH PRAYER

God, show us what gifts and talents we have, and then help us to offer them as best as we can to serve you. We want to be your tools in the world. Use us as you see fit. Amen.

# 35

# THE VALUE OF HARD WORK

## FIND THIS OBJECT

A BAG OF COINS—Or, if you're feeling a little more adventurous, buy some of those chocolate candy coins and hold them over a candle with tongs as you read the story!

## ASK THESE QUESTIONS

Sometimes people talk about learning things "the easy way" or "the hard way." What do you think they mean by that? Which lessons do you typically remember better—those learned the easy way or the hard way? Today's story is about learning an important lesson the hard way.

## BEGIN THE STORY

Once upon a time there was a boy who did not know the value of hard work. He'd grown up in a rich family and was rather lazy, since he didn't have to work. The boy was so lazy that one day his father, who was a very hard worker indeed, sent him off to earn a living. "When you've learned the value of hard work," he told his son. "You can return and be part of our family again."

    The boy left home and found out right away that he did not like to work at all. So after only one week, he returned and asked his mother for some money so that he could show his dad he'd earned something. At first she didn't want to do it, but she finally gave him a bag of coins, for she had missed him and wanted him back home again. Then, the boy returned to his father. "I've learned the value of hard work!" he told his dad.

"In a week?" his dad exclaimed. "Let me see those coins you've earned."

The boy gave his father the bag of coins, and his dad immediately threw them into the fireplace. The boy just stood there staring at his father, trying to figure out what was going on. The fire burned all around the coins, melting some of them and charring the rest. Then, his dad shook his head. "Nope," he said. "You haven't learned the value of hard work yet. Come back home when you have."

So the boy set out again. This time, he returned home still penniless after a month. And once again he begged his mother for some money to prove to his dad that he'd learned what it means to work hard, and once again she gave it to him.

"So," said his father. "Let me see what you've earned in a month." And he took the coins and once again threw them into the fire. The boy watched his dad, just as confused as before.

"Nope," his dad said. "You still don't know. Don't come back until you know the value of hard work. I mean it this time!"

This time the boy left for a year. And this time he got a job working in the fields. He worked from dawn until dusk every day except for Sundays. After a full year of working hard he had earned a small bag of coins. He returned home exhausted, and once again his father met him at the door.

"So, have you learned the value of hard work?" asked his father. The boy nodded and watched as his father took the bag of coins he'd worked so hard to earn and tossed them into the fireplace. But this time, the boy didn't just stand there. Instead, he ran over to the fireplace and began reaching into the fire to pull out the coins before they melted or were damaged. Even though it burned his hands to do so, he couldn't stand the thought of all that money being wasted.

"Yes," said his father. "You have learned the value of hard work. Welcome back, son. You will always be welcome here."

So the boy grew up to become a good manager and a wise leader just like his father. For he had learned a lesson that is hard to learn without living it out for yourself.[7]

## The End

Some of life's mountains are tough to climb;
And only make sense with sweat and time.

## LEARN FROM SCRIPTURE

Why would that boy reach into the fire to get the coins? Why didn't he reach into the fire the first couple times? Here's a question that might seem a little strange: Did the father in the story love his son? If so, why did he keep sending him away from home? Was that a very loving thing to do? What can this story teach you about life?

We all need to watch that we don't become lazy. As it says in the Bible, "Lazybones, how long will you sleep? When will you wake up? I want you to learn this lesson: A little extra sleep, a little more slumber, a little folding of the hands to rest—and poverty will pounce on you like a bandit; scarcity will attack you like an armed robber" (Prov. 6:9–11).

In the New Testament, Paul says that if a man isn't willing to do his share of the work, he doesn't deserve to eat (see 2 Thess. 3:10).

It's easy to let laziness creep up on us. Let's ask God to help us remain watchful, faithful, and careful about the work he gives us to do and to learn the importance of hard work for ourselves.

## END WITH PRAYER

God, sometimes it's tough to learn the value of hard work because we like things to happen the easy way. Use whatever methods you need to teach us the importance of hard work, just like the father did in this story. Amen.

# 36

# THE LAND WITH
# NO MIRRORS

## FIND THIS OBJECT

A MIRROR——Take turns looking into the bathroom mirror and making silly faces. See who can make the weirdest face. Do these faces: proud, stupid, angry, happy, sad, and surprised.

## ASK THESE QUESTIONS

When you look into a mirror, you see your reflection. Is that really how you look? How do you know? Do mirrors serve a good purpose? Do they pose any dangers?

## BEGIN THE STORY

Long ago in the days of knights in shining armor and dragons in the hills, a fourteen-year-old princess named Alexaundra lived at the palace with her parents, the king and the queen. It was a kingdom like many kingdoms in those days; it had blacksmiths and jousting contests and people with really weird wigs. But there was one thing Alexaundra's land did not have—mirrors.

No one in the entire land had ever seen his or her reflection.

One day as Alexaundra was exploring some unused rooms of the castle, she found something round and shiny. When she picked it up by the handle and held it up to her face, she saw a girl's picture in it. *My, what a lovely girl!* she thought at first.

She took it to show her father, the king.

"What do you have there?" he asked her.

"It's a picture of a pretty girl!" said Alexaundra, handing it to him.

Her father took the mirror. "Ha!" he said. "If that's a pretty girl, I'm a Moravian Sea Duck! This isn't a pretty girl. It's the picture of an ugly old man!"

"What?" she cried, taking the mirror from him and looking into it again. "No, Dad, it's a girl!"

He came over and they both looked into it. "Knights of the Round Table!" he cried. "Now I see both a pretty girl who looks a bit like you *and* an ugly old man. It's a picture that changes! It must be magic! Take it to the Imperial Wizard. He'll know what to do with it."

Alexaundra was about to tell her father that the ugly old man in the picture looked a bit like him, but decided against it. Instead, she did as he said and took the mirror to the Imperial Wizard. When he saw it, his eyes grew as large as saucers. "Knights of the Round Table!" he cried. "Where did you get that?"

"In the high tower on the west end of the castle. What is it?"

"It is a truth plate, my dear!"

"A what?"

"A truth plate. When you look into it, it shows you the truth. It reflects back the world as it really is."

Alexaundra looked into the truth plate. "You mean that's me! That's what I look like?"

The wizard nodded. "That's how you look to everyone else." He was gazing into the truth plate himself as he spoke, smoothing out the right side of his beard. "Hmm," he mumbled. "I must have slept on that side."

"Oh, no!" said Alexaundra, looking into it again. "My nose is too big and some of my nose hairs are sticking out. How embarrassing!"

"Mmm," said the wizard peering into the truth plate. "These were outlawed long ago for they can lead to vanity and pride and jealousy. This one must have survived from the days of the previous king."

"But it's such a wonderful thing!" she said, staring into the truth plate, tilting her head and poofing her hair. "It should never be outlawed! Everybody should have one!"

The wizard looked up from the truth plate for a moment and stared off into space. "Or maybe no one should," he said softly. Then, he snatched the truth plate from Alexaundra's hands and smashed it against the floor, shattering it into a thousand pieces.

"What have you done?" cried the princess. And she ran to get her father, the king, who was so angry at the wizard that he sent him to the dungeon for the rest of his days. For when the princess told the king that the man in the truth plate had really been him, he was not in a good mood for six whole days. "I couldn't be that ugly!" he shouted. "Could I?"

And since he was the king, no one was brave enough to answer him.

So while the Imperial Wizard sat in the dungeon, wondering if he'd really done the right thing, the king and all his servants searched the castle from top to bottom for another truth plate.

But thankfully, none were ever found.

## The End

To look in a mirror is to peer at the truth,
Whether close up or from afar.
When you stare in a mirror, then suddenly *poof!*
Something strange and quite bizarre!
A sense of pride. A sense of shame.
As you finally see who you are.

## LEARN FROM SCRIPTURE

What do you think about that story? Did the wizard do a good thing by breaking the only mirror in the land? Why do you say that?

What danger is there in seeing our reflection? What benefits? Can you think of anything that serves as a mirror for your soul?

God's Word shows us that our souls are flawed, imperfect, but deeply loved and graciously forgiven by God.

Psalm 119:104–106 says, "Your commandments give me understanding; no wonder I hate every false way of life. Your word is a lamp for my feet and a light for my path. I've promised it once, and I'll promise again: I will obey your wonderful laws."

As we read the Bible, we see the ugly parts of our souls, but also the beauty of God's matchless love. When God looks at the lives of believers, he sees only his precious children.

## END WITH PRAYER

God, keep us from both pride and jealousy. Instead, show us the deep truths of our lives and draw us closer to you. Amen.

# 37

# MAKING DADDY LOVE ME MORE

## FIND THIS OBJECT

HANDMADE VALENTINES for each member of the family—
Even if it's not close to Valentine's Day, who cares? Go for it.

## ASK THESE QUESTIONS

*(Exchange the Valentine's cards. Encourage each other. Give a group hug. Have a nice little love-fest.)*

Love is a hard thing to understand. Can anyone tell me what love is? What's the definition of love? Can you earn someone's love like you might earn their respect?

As I read today's story, think about how easy (or hard) it is for you to give and receive love.

## BEGIN THE STORY

Once there was a girl named Topeka who loved her dad very much. She knew that he loved her too, but she wanted to make him love her even more. So she decided to try and do things for him so his love for her would grow stronger. *Surely he'll love me more if I obey him all the time!* she thought.

So she obeyed her dad and acted good. She was even nice to her snotty little brother. And while her dad was certainly thankful that she was being obedient, he didn't seem to love her any differently. "Do you love me more now, Daddy?" she asked.

"I already love you with all my heart, sweetie. How could I love you more?"

That made her feel good, but she didn't really believe it. Not really. Certainly there must be something she could do to make him love her more.

The next day, Topeka cleaned her room. She put her dirty clothes in the hamper, neatly arranged her stuffed animals on her pillow, and even swept out the dust bunnies that were underneath her bed—which was quite a job since some were the size of soccer balls. Then she ran up to him and said, "I cleaned my room, Daddy! Do you love me more now?"

"I already told you how much I love you," he said. "How could I love you more?"

The next day, Topeka made a mistake. She punched her brother and made him cry because he wouldn't leave her alone when she was trying to study for her history test. Her brother went and told her dad, who came to talk to Topeka.

"You hit your brother," he said.

"I'm sorry, Dad," she said. By then she was crying too, just like her brother, but not because she was hurt. It was because she was afraid that now her dad wouldn't love her as much as before.

Her father put his hand on her shoulder. "You need to tell your brother that you're sorry, Topeka."

So she did. She told her brother she was sorry, and she meant it a little, though partly she just said it because she had to. Then she came back to her father. "Do you still love me?" she asked, even though she was afraid of the answer.

"Of course," said her father. "I already told you. I love you with all of my heart."

And he held her in his arms and, for the first time, she really believed him.

## The End

God's love can't be earned; he won't be impressed,
He can't love us more and he won't love us less.
Though I don't understand it, I'll never know why—
His love is as full as the span of the sky.

## LEARN FROM SCRIPTURE

How much do you think God loves you? Do you sometimes think he
might love you more if you act good or less if you act bad? Why do you
think we sometimes get caught believing things like that?

Jesus' friend John had a lot to say about loving God and about God's
love for us. He wrote, "We know what real love is because Christ gave up
his life for us" (1 John 3:16). God showed his love for us in this—while we
were still sinners, Christ died for us (see Rom. 5:8). First John 4:16 says,
"We know how much God loves us, and we have put our trust in him. God
is love, and all who live in love live in God, and God lives in them."

We can't earn God's love. We can only believe in it and accept it. Let's
do that right now.

## END WITH PRAYER

God, your love for us is already as full as it could ever be.
Forgive us for the times we've tried to earn your love. Help our
hearts to believe—truly believe—in the depth of your love for
us. Amen.

# 38

# A WOLF IN SHEEP'S CLOTHING

## FIND THIS OBJECT

EITHER A SHIRT you don't want, a mask, or a silly holiday costume—Talk about the different ways that we dress up, hide, or wear costumes—even on days other than holidays. Play dress up if your kids enjoy it.

## ASK THESE QUESTIONS

Sometimes people try to disguise different parts of who they are. Some people try to look thinner or smarter or cooler or richer than they really are. Have you seen people do that? How about you? When do you dress up or wear a costume? What kinds of masks or costumes do people wear? Why would they do that?

## BEGIN THE STORY

Rudy the Wolf struggled with the sheep suit he'd just bought from The Wolf's Howl Costume Supply Company. "With this suit on, no one will ever guess I'm really a wolf!" he said with a grin.

It was a little tough pulling the zipper up over his tummy. "Hmm ... must have put on a little weight there ... too many carbs," he mumbled.

But then he thought of all the sheep he was about to eat and thought, *I'm about to put on a lot more weight!*

Finally he managed to jam his legs into the sheep costume legs and, after a great deal of huffing and puffing and pulling and yanking and sucking in of his tummy, he was able to zip the zipper all the way up to his chin.

It was pretty tough to walk in the sheep suit too, but he managed. After all, he was *very* hungry. At last Rudy made his way over the hill toward the flock of unsuspecting sheep.

"Howl—I mean, Baa," he said to one of the sheep.

"Baa," said the sheep.

"I'm a sheep," said Rudy.

"So I see," said the sheep, staring at the zipper on his suit with big, blank eyes.

"You're not too bright, are you?" said Rudy.

"Baa," said the sheep, and went back to nibbling on her grass.

Rudy smiled, thinking, *This is going to be even easier than I thought!* He licked his chops, opened up his mouth, and was about to gobble down the sheep, when he heard movement behind him.

"Hey!" said a voice. "What are you doing there?"

*Uh-oh,* thought Rudy. He turned around and saw the shepherd standing there holding the stout staff that he used for whacking wolves on the head.

*This might not be good,* thought Rudy.

"Get out of here!" yelled the shepherd. He raised the staff and whacked Rudy soundly on the head. Rudy howled and tried to run away, but it was tough, being zipped up in that sheep suit and all.

Rudy got whacked on the head more times than he could count before he was able to waddle away. And in the end, the sheep were safe, the shepherd was happy, and Rudy lived hungrily ever after.

## *The End*

So here is the moral and the lesson to keep:
You can't trick the shepherd
Though you might fool the sheep.

# LEARN FROM SCRIPTURE

Jesus called his followers sheep and said that he would guide, protect, and lead them. He warned about those people who look like sheep but are really enemies in disguise. They pretend to be believers, but really have no desire to listen to the Good Shepherd. "Watch out for false prophets," said Jesus. "They come to you in sheep's clothing, but inwardly they are ferocious wolves" (Matt. 7:15 NIV).

*(Talk about what it means to be a sheep and what Jesus meant when he talked about ferocious wolves dressing up in sheep's clothes.)*

God sees into the heart and knows who his children are and who is just pretending to be one of his sheep. Let's ask God to help us never to pretend, but always to follow him for real.

# END WITH PRAYER

Jesus, you don't want us to be phony followers or part-time believers. Forgive us for the times we've pretended to be more spiritual than we are. Keep us on the lookout for those who fake being your followers but only want to hurt your sheep. Help us instead to be true worshipers of you, inside and out. Amen.

# 39

# BRENDAN'S BIG DECISION

## FIND THIS OBJECT

A CAMERA—If you have film or a digital camera, take turns taking pictures. Get some silly ones, some serious ones, and some weird ones.

## ASK THESE QUESTIONS

You could take a picture of anything in this room. How did you decide what to take the picture of? Was it tough? Why or why not?

What are some of the things you have to think about when you make a decision?

## BEGIN THE STORY

Brendan the Bass sometimes had a hard time making up his mind. I mean, he could swim in any direction he wanted! He could go up or down; or left or right; or forward or backward; or any which way he pleased. *Ta-da!*

But Brendan had no idea which way he pleased.

One day, his friend Archibald the Walleye swam up. "Whatcha doin', Brendan?"

"Trying to decide which way to go," replied Brendan. "I could go anywhere I please! *Ta-da!*"

"Well, that's true," said Archibald. "It certainly is. No question about that. Well, I'm on my way to play tag with some minnows. Would you like to come?"

Now, Brendan had never played tag with the minnows, but it sounded like great fun. "Yeah!" said Brendan. "I'd love to!"

"Great," said Archibald. "C'mon then!" And Archibald began to swim to the underwater boulder field where the minnows liked to play.

But Brendan just stayed right where he was.

"What's wrong?" asked Archibald, turning around and staring at Brendan. "Aren't you coming?"

"Um, I can't decide if I should swim up or down; or left or right; or forward or backward to come with you."

"Well, just choose one!"

"But it's so hard."

"No, it's not! Just move. Remember, *ta-da?*"

But Brendan didn't move. Archibald waited a few more minutes, but finally he got tired of waiting for Brendan to decide. "I can't wait all day, Brendan, or the game will be over," he said. "See you later, alligator."

"Alligator! Where?" cried Brendan, scared he might actually have to decide where to swim after all.

"It's just a saying, Brendan." Then Archibald swam off to play with the minnows. "Bye, Brendan. I'll see you later."

"See you later," said Brendan, staying in the same place in the water. *I'd sure like to play tag!* he thought as he looked around. *Maybe I should swim up, no, down … no, to my left … no, I better go right … or maybe backward, but why not just forward? Oh, phooey! I don't know where to go!*

So he didn't go anywhere.

And then summer ended and fall came and fall ended and winter came and with the winter, the cold, cold weather. And of course, the lake froze in the frigid air and the ice formed all around Brendan the Bass so that he couldn't swim anywhere at all, even if he'd wanted to. And as far as I know, he's still there today, stuck in that lake.

But of course it didn't really matter, because he wasn't going anywhere anyway.

## *The End*

Choices take courage, for it's easy to stay
In the same exact place or to act the same way.
So to move ahead, well, we need to be bold,
Or we'll be stuck where we are until we get old.

## LEARN FROM SCRIPTURE

Would it really have mattered which direction Brendan chose to swim? Do you ever get stuck like he did, trying to make a decision that doesn't really matter all that much in the end? How can you change that?

What are some of the choices you have to make every day? How much do they matter? What would it be like if you were never able to make any decisions at all?

Ecclesiastes 11:4 says, "If you wait for perfect conditions, you will never get anything done." It's true that if we wait for everything to be perfect we'll never accomplish anything. It takes boldness to make a decision, to make a change. Some decisions are important and require great wisdom. So to make the right decisions, we need both boldness and wisdom.

James 1:5 reminds us, "If you need wisdom—if you want to know what God wants you to do—ask him, and he will gladly tell you. He will not resent your asking." Let's ask God to give us the wisdom to make good choices and the courage to see them through to the end.

## END WITH PRAYER

God, help us to make both big decisions and little ones with wisdom. Then help us to have the courage to act on our decisions even if the conditions don't seem to be quite perfect yet. Amen.

# 40

# The Tale of the Brat and the Goody Two-Shoes

## Find This Object

Walk around the house and pick up stuff that's lying around on the floor. Put the stuff you've gathered onto the table before beginning to read the story. Talk about how nobody wants to pick up after themselves. Do you usually do so when you're told to? Why or why not?

## Ask These Questions

Think of a time when a teacher or a parent asked you to do something and you said you'd do it, but then you didn't. Does anyone want to tell us the story of what happened?

*(Allow them to respond.)*

Sometimes we do that with God. We find out he wants us to do something, and we tell him we'll do it, but then we change our minds and don't follow through. That's partly what this story is about.

## Begin the Story

Once there were two brothers. One of them always did what was wrong. And when he did, he would always say this to his dad *(read these refrains with rhythm):*

"I'm not gonna do it, no, I'm not gonna do,
No, I'm not gonna do what you want me to!"

The other brother always did what was right, and when he did, he
would say this to his dad:

"I'm-a gonna do it, yeah, I'm-a gonna do,
Yeah, I'm-a gonna do what you want me to!"

So one day, their dad said to the first boy, "I want you to clean your
room!" And so the boy said to his dad:

"I'm not gonna do it, no, I'm not gonna do,
No, I'm not gonna do what you want me to!"

And then, their dad told the other boy, "I want you to clean your room
too!" And so, of course, that boy said:

"I'm-a gonna do it, yeah, I'm-a gonna do,
Yeah, I'm-a gonna do what you want me to!"

But during the day, the first boy changed his mind. You remember
him, right? He was the one who liked to say:

"I'm not gonna do it, no, I'm not gonna do,
No, I'm not gonna do what you want me to!"

Well, now he said:

"I'm-a gonna do it, yeah, I'm-a gonna do,
Yeah, I'm-a gonna do what you want me to!"

And he went and cleaned up his room.

But his brother, the one who'd agreed at first changed his mind too.
You remember him—he's the one who always said:

"I'm-a gonna do it, yeah, I'm-a gonna do,
Yeah, I'm-a gonna do what you want me to!"

Well, he decided not to obey after all. He thought to himself:

*I'm not gonna do it, no, I'm not gonna do,*
*No, I'm not gonna do what you want me to!*

And at the end of the day, one of those boys got a spanking and was
grounded from playing video games for the rest of the week. I wonder if
you can guess which one it was. And can you guess which boy got to eat
hot, buttery popcorn and watch a movie with his dad before going to bed
that night? You're right. And that's why ...

## The End

It's always better to find your way
Toward following God and learning to obey,
Than promising to do what Jesus has said,
But going a different direction instead.

## LEARN FROM SCRIPTURE

Jesus told a story just like this one. And when he was done telling it, he explained that even those who haven't lived good lives can enter God's kingdom when they believe in him and change their minds to begin following God's ways.

*(Read and explore Matthew 21:28–32.)*

Believing in Jesus and following him go hand in hand. Jesus accepts us when we begin to trust in God and live for him. He forgives us for all the wrongs we've done and gives us a place in the kingdom of heaven. Let's pray that God helps us to say:

"I'm-a gonna do it, yeah, I'm-a gonna do,
Yeah, I'm-a gonna do what you want me to!"

Even if we used to tell him:

"I'm not gonna do it, no, I'm not gonna do,
No, I'm not gonna do what you want me to!"

It's never too late to start walking in the ways of Jesus.

## END WITH PRAYER

*(Encourage your children to join you in saying this refrain to God.*
*I'm-a gonna do it, yeah, I'm-a gonna do,*
*Yeah, I'm-a gonna do what you want me to!)*

God, you're looking for people who do more than promise to live for you. You want people who really do follow you. Help us to trust in you and walk in your ways, even if we've failed to do so in the past. Amen.

# 41

# THE LEOPARD
# AND THE VILLAGERS

## FIND THIS OBJECT

AN ACORN OR A PINECONE—*(Please note: Since a boy dies at the end of this story, use your best judgment when deciding whether or not to read it to younger children. This story may only be appropriate for families with older kids.)*

## ASK THESE QUESTIONS

Can you think of something that starts out small and easy to handle, but soon grows so big or strong that it's hard to control? *(Pull out the acorn.)* This is one thing that does that. What is it? What does it grow into? Can you think of little choices in your life that lead to bigger and bigger ones?

Today's story comes from far away but the lesson it teaches hits close to home.

## BEGIN THE STORY

Long ago in a village near the jungle there lived a boy who liked to explore. One day when he was walking through the jungle, he found a baby leopard. The boy thought it would make a great pet. "I'll take it home and raise it as my own!" he said to himself.

But when he carried the leopard back into the village, his uncle saw it and warned the boy, "Take that leopard back into the jungle and set it free, for one day it will grow large and powerful, and you won't be able to control it anymore."

"No," said the boy. "Don't worry. I'll be careful." And the rest of the people in the town agreed, for the leopard looked small and cute and quite harmless.

His uncle shook his head and said, "I'm telling you, little leopards grow into big leopards, and big leopards kill."

In time, the baby leopard grew and soon it was chasing the dogs and cats around the village. One day a dog was found dead at the edge of the village and, although no one knew for sure, they suspected the leopard had done it.

"It's not too late," said the boy's uncle. "You can still get rid of the leopard before it gets too big. Take it back to the jungle. Let it go! Little leopards grow into big leopards, and big leopards kill!"

But the boy didn't listen to his uncle. Instead, he kept feeding the leopard, and indeed it did grow bigger and stronger and more and more fierce. And one terrible day it turned on the boy and attacked him, and the boy did not survive. All the villagers had to band together to drive the fierce leopard from their village, for now they were all in danger.

At the boy's funeral, his uncle couldn't stop crying. And some people remembered hearing him say over and over again, "Little leopards grow into big leopards, and big leopards kill."[8]

## The End

Little temptations don't stay small;
By feeding them they grow stronger and tall.
Sin always wants to control our needs,
And lead to more and more evil deeds.

## LEARN FROM SCRIPTURE

James 1:14–15 says, "Temptation comes from the lure of our own evil desires. These evil desires lead to evil actions, and evil actions lead to death." Little temptations grow into bigger ones. Little sins grow into bigger sins, and one day those will lead to ruin and destruction.

It works the other way, too. If we obey in the little things, we'll soon learn that the big things aren't quite so big. It'll become easier and easier to follow God in the big areas too.

Let's ask God to help us find the areas of our lives where we're feeding our baby leopards, and then let's stop feeding them and let them go.

## End with Prayer

God, sometimes we think little sins are okay. Forgive us for that. Show us instead how dangerous they are. Help us to release our baby leopards before they grow too big to control. Amen.

# 42

# THE PARABLE OF THE CRAYONS

## FIND THIS OBJECT

A SHOVEL——Talk about the kinds of things you might want to bury or uncover with a shovel. If you like, bury a crayon in your yard or flower bed to reinforce the lesson from this story.

## ASK THESE QUESTIONS

Why would you bury something valuable? What are the different ways people bury the gifts, talents, and resources God gives them? Why do you think people do that?

## BEGIN THE STORY

One day a mother had to go into her kitchen to answer the phone, so she left her three daughters in the living room to color. She left the oldest girl with five crayons, the middle daughter with two crayons, and the youngest child with one crayon. Then she went to talk on the phone.

As soon as she left, the oldest girl took her five crayons and, by shading them together on her page, was able to make five brand new colors! The middle daughter took her two crayons and, by shading them together, was able to make two new colors!

The youngest daughter was mad that she only got one crayon. She stuck out her lower lip and took her crayon and broke it up into little bitty pieces.

Soon their mother returned to look at the pictures her children had colored while she was gone. The oldest daughter ran up to her mother waving her picture. "Look, Mommy!" she cried. "I used the five crayons you gave me and created five new colors!"

"Nice!" said her mother with a smile. "You did well with the crayons I left you. Because of that I'm going to give you a 64-pack of crayons with one of those little sharpening things in the side of it!"

"Cool!" said the oldest daughter.

Then the middle daughter showed her mother the picture she'd colored. "Look, Mom! I used the two colors you gave me, and I made two new colors by shading them together!"

"Very nice!" said her mother. "You did well with the crayons I left you. Because of that I'm going to give you a 48-pack of crayons that includes two new never-before-seen glow-in-the-dark colors!"

"All right!" said the middle daughter. "You rock, Mom!"

Then, the mother turned to the youngest daughter who was sitting on the floor with her lower lip stuck out and her arms folded. "And what about you?" she asked her daughter.

"Humph!" said the youngest girl. "I didn't think it was fair that you gave them more than you gave me. So I broke my crayon into bits!"

"Well, I guess you ended up with even less than you started with," said her mother.

"Don't I get some new crayons too?" she cried.

"Nope," her mother answered. "And because of the way you're acting, you don't get any ice cream for dessert, either." Then the mother scooped out two big bowls of Neapolitan ice cream for her two oldest daughters and put the pictures they'd colored on the refrigerator. And the youngest daughter ran off to her room, where there was weeping and gnashing of teeth.

## *The End*

The gifts that God gives us are meant to be used,
Not wasted, neglected, forgotten, or abused.
Though our gifts and our talents might seem tiny or small,
God will use them well when we give him our all.

# LEARN FROM SCRIPTURE

Which girl, or girls, do you think Jesus would want us to be more like? Why? Do you know which one of Jesus' stories this one is similar to? *(Read or retell Matthew 25:14–30.)* What could Jesus have meant by telling a story like that? What do you think God wants you to do with the time, money, imagination, ideas, dreams, and talents he has given you?

God wants us to use all we have to help expand his kingdom. What are some ways people waste (or bury) their talents today? If you've buried the ideas, talents, or gifts God has given you, it's time to uncover them once again and use them to serve him. Let's ask him to help us do that right now.

# END WITH PRAYER

God, help us to risk, trust, and serve you with all we are and all we have. Sometimes we're tempted to just hide our gifts away, but help us instead to step out in faith and do all we can to help your kingdom grow. Amen.

## 43

# THAT STINKY, SKUNKY STUFF

## FIND THIS OBJECT

A PLUNGER

## ASK THESE QUESTIONS

What things make you want to yell or scream? When do you find yourself yelling the most? Does yelling usually help, or does it make things worse? *(Hold up the plunger.)* What do you use this for? Is it a messy, stinky job? Can you think of anything that smells even worse?

Today's story is about a little skunk with a big problem.

## BEGIN THE STORY

Skunk had a short temper. Whenever anyone got in his way or got on his nerves or didn't give him something he wanted, he would spray them with his stinky, skunky stuff. "Take that!" he would say as he blasted away. "That'll teach you!"

And, as you can imagine, it wasn't long before all the other forest animals left Skunk alone and wanted nothing to do with him. "We don't want to play with you!" they'd say from a safe distance. "Or you'll spray us!"

"You bet I will!" said Skunk with a grin. "If you get me angry! But who cares? I didn't want to play with you anyway!" And then he would go off to play by himself. He was a very rude and impatient fellow.

One afternoon he became especially angry. He sprayed the root of a tree which he accused of trying to trip him. He sprayed a rock for being in his way, and he even sprayed the ground because it was too sandy. "Take that! And that! And that!" he yelled. He would have sprayed the sun for being so hot but it was too far away.

That evening just after dusk, a great horned owl—one of the only animals brave enough to eat skunks—settled onto a branch high above him to watch.

"Hi," said the owl.

"Go away," said Skunk. "Or I'll blast you!"

"You've been doing a lot of spraying," said Owl.

"So what?"

"So I think you might be out of your stinky, skunky stuff," said Owl. Skunk hadn't thought of that. "So what if I am?"

"So I've been thinking of having you for dinner," said Owl.

"No thanks, I'm not hungry."

"But I am," said Owl as she swooped down to snatch up Skunk. He tried to spray her, but he was indeed out of stinky, skunky stuff. Thankfully, though, Skunk was quick enough to scurry into a dead stump where he waited, in a rather cramped position, all night long until finally Owl flew away.

And that next day, Skunk was very stiff and sore from being stuck in the stump. He had also become so frightened of Owl that he'd sprayed himself. "This really stinks," he said. And he was right.

He wished he could go and talk to someone about it, but everyone ran away whenever he came near.

And Skunk decided it would be better next time to save up his stinky, skunky stuff for a time when he really needed it. And so, he was a much more patient fellow from then on.

## The End

Despite what some may say or think,
Short, angry tempers really stink.
Patience is always a better choice;
Rude, angry people rarely rejoice.

# LEARN FROM SCRIPTURE

Being patient rather than quick-tempered is a fruit of the Spirit. That means it grows naturally when God's Spirit is guiding us and working in our lives. Proverbs 12:16 says "a fool is quick-tempered." What makes it hard to be patient sometimes? When are you the most tempted to lose your temper? What are you going to do about it?

James, the brother of Jesus, gives us this advice on getting along: "My dear brothers and sisters, be quick to listen, slow to speak, and slow to get angry. Your anger can never make things right in God's sight" (James 1:19–20).

God doesn't get angry easily. In fact, Psalm 103:8 says, "He is slow to get angry and full of unfailing love."

Let's ask God to help us become more like him and less like Skunk.

# END WITH PRAYER

God, being mad all the time really stinks. Help us not to be so angry and rude, but rather patient with each other, just as you are patient with us. Amen.

# 44

# POISON IVY IN THE FLOWER BED

## FIND THIS OBJECT

A BOTTLE OF POISON IVY CREAM or first-aid lotion

## ASK THESE QUESTIONS

Have you ever had poison ivy? Or have you known someone who has? What's it like? What should you do when you see a poison ivy plant? Let's listen to what Terry did when he found some poison ivy in his mother's flower bed.

## BEGIN THE STORY

One bright spring day Terry ran out to the flower bed to pick some flowers for his mother. But he gasped when he saw that growing right next to the flowers was a big bunch of the bright, shiny, three-leafed plants his mother had warned him never to touch.

Last week, pointing to similar plants in the woods, Terry's mom had told him, "That's poison ivy. If you touch it you'll be sorry. You'll be itching for a long time!"

So when he saw it in the flower bed, Terry ran inside and said, "Mom! Dad! Guess what? Poison ivy is growing in the flower bed!"

"Oh, my," said his mother. "Not next to my petunias!"

"Yes, next to your petunias. I went to pick you some flowers, but I was afraid I might touch the poison ivy and get all itchy." Terry thought for a moment. Then he grinned. "Should we spray some poison on it to kill it?"

"I don't think so," said his mother.

"Maybe attack it with a high-powered, six-cylinder engine, torque-controlled weed whacker with razor sharp blades?"

"Probably not a good idea," said his dad. "You'd get poison ivy leaves all over you."

"Pour acid on it?"

"Goodness, no!" said his mother.

"That's right," said his dad. "Listen to your mother. No acid. After all, you might get some on your foot and it would burn right through your shoe, land on your skin, and begin to melt its way down to the bone and—"

"Um, I think that's enough, dear," Terry's mother interrupted.

"Oh, Mom!" said Terry. "He was just getting to the good part!"

"No more talk of acid," said his mother.

"How about bombs then?" said Terry. "Could we maybe blow it up?"

"Um, that would be a no" said his dad. "We'd end up blowing up all the flowers, too. Not to mention the house."

"Cool," said Terry.

"Not cool," said his mother.

"Then what'll we do?" asked Terry.

"We'll let them grow together this summer," said his dad, "and then next fall, when the leaves are gone and I can see what I'm doing, I'll pull up the poison ivy by the roots so it won't grow in the flower bed next year or ever again."

So, after summer passed, Terry's dad did just that. He went out with his garden tools and gloves and pulled up all the poison ivy by the roots and burned it in a big bonfire. He even let Terry light the match. "I know it's not as good as blowing up the house, but at least it's something," he said.

"Yeah," said Terry. "But I still like the acid idea best."

Then his dad took Terry's hand. "We need to go inside while it burns or we'll breathe in the poison ivy fumes and the poison will coat our throats and lungs and—"

"That's enough, dear!" yelled Terry's mom, who had stepped outside to check on them. Terry smiled at his dad and his dad winked at Terry.

The next spring only flowers grew in the flower bed. And even though he was a little bummed that he couldn't blow anything up, Terry was excited that he could safely pick a bouquet of flowers for his mom. And Terry's family lived happily ever after without any acid burning through the flesh of their feet.

## *The End*

Evil grows in our world right next to the good
And God could destroy it, we know that he could,
But he's biding his time till everything's right—
One day he'll send all that is bad from his sight.

## LEARN FROM SCRIPTURE

*(Read Jesus' parable of the wheat and the weeds found in Matthew 13:24–30.)*
In Jesus' story, can you guess who is like God? Who are the believers? Unbelievers? What about in the story about the poison ivy?

Jesus often told stories about separating believers from unbelievers. His point is that he knows who we are—whether we are his followers or not. We may wonder why God doesn't just destroy all evil. What does Jesus' story tell us about that?

In the story, the men left the bad plants growing next to the good, not to hurt the good plants but to make sure they weren't damaged. God has his reasons for letting evil stay in our world for the time being. One day he will burn it all away.

Let's ask him to show us where we fit into his story and how he wants us to grow closer to him right now.

## END WITH PRAYER

God, help us become flowers of your kingdom, not poison ivy plants! Remind us that you're in charge and one day you'll get rid of evil forever. Until then, help us to be faithful. Amen.

# 45

# THE QUEEN OF THE MERMAIDS

## FIND THIS OBJECT

A PHOTO ALBUM——Talk about emotions, special times, or memories you've shared together. Try to find and relive good memories.

## ASK THESE QUESTIONS

Sometimes terrible things happen that separate families. People have to go to war, sometimes people die, sometimes people get divorced, or children run away.

And sometimes, someone drifts away from the family even though they are still staying under the same roof.

## BEGIN THE STORY

The Queen of the Mermaids had two daughters. The older daughter worked hard every day at pleasing her mother—sometimes planning surprise parties using minnows like confetti, other times teaching the mermaid maids to dance among the sea grass in the courtyard of the underwater palace.

The younger daughter was lazy and greedy. One day she swam up to her mother. "I'm sick and tired of splashing around this stupid coral reef all the time and living on this side of the ocean. If you were to die, I'd get your golden crown and silver rings for each of my fingers, right?"

"Yes, if I were to die," said the queen.

"Well, I don't want to wait around that long!" said the little mermaid. "Give me that stuff now so I can enjoy it while I'm still young."

The queen was saddened by her daughter's request. She feared her daughter might leave home and never come back. But, she loved her so much that she gave her both the gifts that she asked for, and the freedom to leave, if that's what she really wanted.

And as it turns out, it was what she really wanted. As soon as the little mermaid had the golden crown and silver rings, she swam away from home.

Her older sister just shook her head. "I knew she'd turn out to be no good. I would never treat Mother like that." And then she went to work gathering up starfish to put up a mural on the castle wall to impress her mother.

Well, that little mermaid ventured far out into the ocean. Sometimes she would trade a silver ring to an octopus for a back rub or give one to an eel for a dainty fish for supper. She even gave her golden crown to a dolphin for protecting her while she swam through shark-infested waters.

One day she realized she was on the far side of the ocean without any friends or family around, and she had lost all that her mother had given her. She was lonely and tired and hungry, but still very lazy. *Hmm,* she thought. *My mother hires groupers to serve meals in the palace and even they have something to eat each night. Maybe I should go back home and ask her to hire me. It'd be easy work and good food.*

So the little mermaid swam home—not so much because she was sorry for losing her precious rings and crown, or even for breaking her mother's heart, but because she was hungry and didn't know where else to turn.

From a distance her mother saw her, for she'd been watching for her every day at the window of the palace. When she saw her daughter she swam out to meet her—even though greeting visitors was usually the job of the barracudas, or at least the kindly old sea bass named Wilfred. But the Queen of the Mermaids didn't care what people thought of her. She just wanted to see her daughter again.

As the queen threw her arms around her daughter, the little mermaid said, "Mother, I lost the rings and crown you gave me—"

But she couldn't even finish her sentence before her mother interrupted, "I don't care about those. I only care about you."

"Can I maybe serve food with the groupers?"

"Absolutely not!" her mother said. "You're a daughter of the Queen of the Mermaids! You shall sit at the table by my side, where you belong! Tonight we celebrate your return!"

And so the queen held a great party to welcome her daughter home. The crabs danced, the sea urchins sang, and the sea horses swam through everyone's hair. And the only mermaid in the entire sea who refused to come in was the little mermaid's older sister, who just sat on a sponge near the edge of the reef pouting, until finally the queen herself swam over to invite her in.

But still she wouldn't go. "Look, Mom!" said the older daughter. "I make murals for you. I teach the mermaid maids how to dance among the sea grass in the courtyard of the palace, and do you ever reward me? No. Do you ever throw me a party? I don't think so! But now this daughter of yours wastes all that you gave her and you throw her a party?!"

"But your sister was lost and alone at the far side of the ocean," said the queen. "She was as good as dead. But now she's safe. She's home. Don't you understand—we had to have a party!"

"Humph," said the older daughter.

At last the queen shrugged. "Well, suit yourself then. You can stay out here if you like. We'll be inside. Watch out for sharks."

And so everyone in the underwater kingdom celebrated the return of the little mermaid except for her older sister who just folded her arms and said "Humph" and stared past the castle into the inky black water, watching nervously for sharks.

## The End

The gate is wide open, the party's begun,
For all who have wandered and all who have run—
"Come home!" is the message. "Come home and come in!
Come sit at the table, let the singing begin!"

## LEARN FROM SCRIPTURE

Think about this statement and see if you agree or disagree: Both of those daughters were lost, but in different ways. Can you figure out what that might mean?

When it comes to us and God, which mermaid do you think God is most like? What about you? In what ways are you like the older mermaid? In what ways are you like the younger one?

*(If desired, read or review Jesus' story about the two lost sons, found in Luke 15:11–32.)*

God welcomes us home—sometimes after we have run from him, other times when we have drifted from him. But in either case, he is willing and waiting to forgive us and welcome us home again.

## END WITH PRAYER

God, even if our hearts aren't pure and our motives are mixed up, we want to come home. Forgive us for the times we've drifted or run or swam to the far side of your love. Reassure us that you will welcome us back once again. Amen.

# 46

# The Voice of the Wind

## Find This Object

YOUR BREATH——All you'll need for this devotion is your own breath, so you might want to brush your teeth or gargle to make sure your breath smells minty fresh!

To start out, smell each other's breath! (Or you may want to make some music by blowing on a flute or a recorder. This might be a better tie-in for younger children, but it might give away too much of the story for older kids.)

## Ask These Questions

Unless we're standing outside in the winter, our breath is invisible. How can you tell it's real? Think about the wind. Can you see (or smell) the wind? Is the wind visible or invisible? If the wind is invisible, how do you know it's really there?

## Begin the Story

Wind was sad. For unlike Sunset, Wind had no color. And unlike Bird, Wind had no song. And unlike Lake, Wind could not reflect the sun or the moon or the stars. God had not given Wind a color or a face or a song.

And so Wind was sad—partly because he had no color; partly because he had no face, but mostly because he had no song.

As Wind grew from a baby breeze into a mature gust, he went through some tough times. In fact, some people said that during his teenage years he was rather like a tornado. And come to think of it, they were right. But through all of that learning and growing, rushing and blowing, twirling and swirling and spinning around, Wind still had no song. And he was still unhappy.

Wind had grown up on the prairies of Kansas, but when he was old enough he moved to the cliffs in the high mountains of Montana.

One day as he was blowing through the trees that grew along the edge of a vast cliff, he heard beautiful music trailing behind him.

"It must be some fantastic and rare bird!" said Wind, and he slowed down so that he could hear the music better or perhaps catch a glimpse of the beautiful bird in flight. But the slower he went the fainter the music became until finally, as he sat on a mossy tree stump to listen, the music stopped altogether.

*Hmm, it must have been my imagination,* he thought and started on his way once again. But as he did, Wind heard the music again. The faster he went and the more he looked for it, the more he heard the music behind him! *What's going on?* thought Wind. *Who's making that noise?*

He went as fast as he could through the forest, whisking through the feathery branches of the trees and then gliding across the face of a granite cliff. And the music followed him everywhere! It was wonderfully eerie and mysterious. It sounded like the song of a lovely bird mixed with the moan of a lonely coyote.

*What is making that music?* thought Wind. *It must be a truly amazing creature!*

Wind searched and searched, but he never could find the source of the music.

And some people say Wind is still searching along those cliffs and in those forests today. They say that if you go there and listen at just the right time of day, you can hear him searching and you can tell right where he is, even though he's still invisible and has no color or face. Because when Wind searches for the music, he is no longer silent but actually becomes part of the song.

## *The End*

You may never understand the role that you play
In the story God is telling the world today.
But as long as you do what he made you to do,
He'll continue to bless other people through you.

## LEARN FROM SCRIPTURE

Think about that story and Wind's search for the source of that song. What do you think was making the music? What clues told you that? Why was Wind still unhappy? Did he need to be unhappy? What does this story teach us about our lives?

Sometimes we become unhappy when we think God hasn't given us special gifts or the same strengths he's given someone else, even though all the while he is doing amazing things through our lives.

Sometimes our lives and choices impact other people in ways we don't even realize. In Bible times, some people were arguing about who was more important when it came to telling God's story. Paul reminded the people that we all have a role to play and that what really matters isn't our job, but that we keep working together in serving God and spreading his story. He talks about God's story as if it were seeds growing in people's hearts: "The ones who do the planting or watering aren't important, but God is important because he is the one who makes the seed grow. The one who plants and the one who waters work as a team with the same purpose. Yet they will be rewarded individually, according to their own hard work. We work together as partners who belong to God. You are God's field, God's building—not ours" (1 Cor. 3:7–9).

Let's pray that God reminds us how important our lives are, even when we don't see or understand how he is using us.

## END WITH PRAYER

God, I can't always see or understand your ways. Sometimes I never even see the great things you're doing through my life. Encourage me to keep going. And when I hear your music trail behind me, help me to see my place in the song. Amen.

# 47

# LUCY THE CHICKEN

## FIND THIS OBJECT

AN UNFINISHED PROJECT—You might point out a half-finished bookshelf in the workshop, a pile of half-folded laundry in the living room, or a homework assignment your children haven't completed yet.

## ASK THESE QUESTIONS

Have you ever started a job and then quit before it was completed? Why did you stop working on it? Why do you think some people speed up and others slow down when they get close to the finish line in a race? Some people have a tough time getting started; others have a tough time completing things. Which is more like you? Which do you think is more important—starting or finishing something?

## BEGIN THE STORY

*(Note, you may wish to practice reading this story once or twice by yourself before reading it to your family. Have fun creating silly voices for each of the different animals. Remember to keep them all straight!)*

Lucy the Chicken was walking along the side of the road when

155

suddenly ... *Bonk!* Something white and hard and round fell from the sky and clonked her right on the head.

"Ouch!" cried Lucy, rubbing her head and picking up the white, round, hard thing. "It's too dry to be rain, it's too big to be snow, it's too warm to be ice ... it must be a piece of the sky!" Lucy the Chicken put the piece of the sky into her pocket and yelled, "The sky is falling! It's falling! It's falling! The sky is falling down!"

And she ran and she ran and she ran some more, until she came to Moo-Moo the Cow.

"The sky is falling!" Lucy said. "It's falling! It's falling! The sky is falling down!"

"Moo! Moo!" said Moo-Moo. "Oh, no! Where will we go?"

"You gotta follow me to where it's safe below—in a cave!" answered Lucy.

So, the cow followed the chicken. And they ran and they ran and they ran some more until they came to Neigh-Neigh the Horse.

Lucy said, "The sky is falling! It's falling! It's falling! The sky is falling down!"

"Neigh! Neigh! Oh, no! Where will we go?" asked Neigh-Neigh.

"You gotta follow me to where it's safe below—in a cave!"

So, the horse followed the cow, and the cow followed the chicken, and they ran and they ran and they ran some more until they came to Meow-Meow the Kitten ... and then Woof-Woof the Dog ... and then Oink-Oink the Hippo. And each time Lucy said, "The sky is falling! It's falling! It's falling! The sky is falling down!"

And each time the animals said, "Meow, meow!" or "Woof, woof!" or "Oink, oink! Oh, no! Where will we go?"

"You gotta follow me to where it's safe below—in a cave!" answered Lucy the Chicken.

And so at last, the hippo followed the dog, and the dog followed the kitten, and the kitten followed the horse, and the horse followed the cow, and the cow followed the chicken, and they ran and they ran and they ran some more until they came to the cave.

It was a dark, spooky, ooky cave—a cool, wet, windy cave with strange noises coming from inside of it.

"You gotta follow me to where it's safe below—in a cave," mumbled Lucy the Chicken. But she didn't sound so confident anymore.

And the chicken looked at the cow, and the cow looked at the horse, and the horse looked at the kitten, and the kitten looked at the dog, and the dog looked at the hippo, and the hippo looked at the cave. And they all began to shake with fear, knocking their knees together and biting their pawnails or wingtips.

"Do we really need to go in there?" they all asked Lucy.

Suddenly, a creature appeared at the mouth of the cave. It had scales and wings and it breathed out ... whoosh! ... fire! It was a ... *(pause and let the children yell out their guess)*. That's right! A dragon! And he was dressed up in a baseball outfit. He had a bat in one claw and a glove on the other.

"Has anybody seen my baseball?" he asked.

And the hippo looked at the dog, and the dog looked at the kitten, and the kitten looked at the horse, and the horse looked at the cow, and the cow looked at the chicken, and Lucy looked in her pocket. She reached in and pulled out the piece of the sky.

"Um, is this your baseball, Mr. Dragon?" she asked.

"No, that's a piece of the sky!" said the dragon. And at that moment there was a tremendous crash, and the rest of the sky fell on the dragon and the hippo and the dog and the kitten and the horse and the cow and the chicken, squashing them all like grapes—all because they stood around wasting time when they could have gone into the safety of the cave.

## *The End*

So the moral of the story, as you can plainly see
Is that when you've nearly reached the goal
That you've pursued persistently,
Don't lose your focus; finish the task you've begun
Or you'll end up in worse shape than what you started from.

## LEARN FROM SCRIPTURE

Were you surprised by the ending of this story? What kind of lessons do you think this story can teach us? The Bible reminds us to keep our eyes on Jesus and our hearts focused on heaven. "Look straight ahead, and fix your eyes on what lies before you. Mark out a straight path for your feet;

then stick to the path and stay safe. Don't get sidetracked; keep your feet from following evil" (Prov. 4:25–27). And Solomon wrote, "Finishing is better than starting. Patience is better than pride" (Eccl. 7:8).

But sometimes we can get distracted from doing that. What are some of the things that might distract us from following Jesus' teachings or storing up treasures in heaven?

Near the end of his life, Paul wrote, "I have finished the race, and I have remained faithful" (2 Tim. 4:7). Staying faithful to God until the end is the goal of all believers. Let's ask God to help us stay focused on our goal of living for Jesus and not get sidetracked or distracted by other things.

## END WITH PRAYER

God, I want to keep my heart focused on you and what's most important to you. Please help me remember to never give up— either when the goal seems close by or very far away. Amen.

# 48

# HUMBLE CLOTHES

## FIND THIS OBJECT

IF POSSIBLE, DO SOME PEOPLE-WATCHING at the mall or at another public place.

Try to guess what other people might do for a living based on how they're dressed, how they talk, or what they wear. Try to guess if they're rich or poor, happy or sad. Have fun. Get weird.

## ASK THESE QUESTIONS

What message do your clothes give? Can you tell anything about a person by how they dress or what kind of car they drive? Keep that in mind as I read this story.

## BEGIN THE STORY

A student was sitting with her teacher when she saw a rich woman walk past. The student pointed and said, "I've heard that woman is very humble."

But the teacher shook his head. "Look how she's dressed in the latest and most expensive clothes. See her cool shoes? Her stylin' haircut? Her nicely coordinated ensemble with trendy accessories?"

"Yeah," said the student, wishing she could look that good.

"Well, humble people don't dress like that because they don't want to be noticed. They don't want people to admire them. They don't try to make a good impression or get people to look up to them."

"They don't?"

"No."

"Oh," said the student. "Why not?"

"Because they would rather make an accurate impression than a good one."

"Oh," said the student. "I don't get it."

Just then, a man dressed in rags walked past. "Then that must be a truly humble man," said the student. "I know him, and he could afford much nicer clothes. He's not showing off or anything. Instead, he pretty much looks like a slob. Sort of like a walking yard sale."

"Wrong again," said the teacher. "Well, you're right about the slob part, but he's calling attention to how poorly he's dressed. He's showing off in a different way. Rather than show us what he could *buy* for himself, he's showing us what he can *deny* himself. The humble person doesn't call attention to himself at all, in either direction."

"Then how do truly humble people act and dress?" asked the confused student.

"That is the question we all need to answer," said the teacher.

## *The End*

Rather than show off and try to impress
By the way that you act and the way that you dress,
Strive to be humble, rather than proud,
Don't try to stand out from the rest of the crowd.

## LEARN FROM SCRIPTURE

Why do you think Paul would write to the Christians of his day, "Don't be selfish; don't live to make a good impression on others. Be humble, thinking of others as better than yourself" (Phil. 2:3)? Why would he tell them not to try and make a good impression? Did Jesus ever try to make a good impression or just an accurate one?

What do you think—can you tell how humble a person is by what they wear? Jesus explained that humble people don't try to exalt themselves. That means they don't try to show off, build themselves up, or do things just to get attention. Have you seen people exalt themselves? Does it make you think they're more humble or less humble? How do you think humble people act and dress and talk? Can you guess why humility is so important to God?

# END WITH PRAYER

God, teach me how to be more humble. Amen.

# 49

# THE BRAGGING FOX

## FIND THIS OBJECT

A TOOTHBRUSH—Talk about what you use a toothbrush for: It cleans your teeth. Is there anything that can clean out the words in your mouth?

## ASK THESE QUESTIONS

Are you ever tempted to talk about someone behind his back? Like, maybe when you're on the phone and you start to talk about someone who's not there in the room. As you listen to today's story, see which of the characters you are the most like.

## BEGIN THE STORY

Once there was a fox who loved to talk about himself all the time. Whenever the other animals invited him over for dinner or to a ball game or even to go out to a movie, he would spend the whole time talking about what he'd done. "I'm not trying to brag or anything," he would say, "but last week I escaped the hunters in a most clever way …" And then he would tell them all about how brave, smart, witty, and handsome he was.

Of course you can imagine that, in time, Fox found himself being invited out less and less by the other animals.

In fact, after awhile all the other animals except for Toad left Fox alone. But Toad would sit and listen to Fox for hours. For some reason he seemed to enjoy listening to Fox.

"How do you put up with him?" the other animals asked, shaking their heads. "He's always talking about himself! Always bragging and carrying on!"

"Yes, that he does," said Toad, "and then I come here and you talk about him. Honestly, I'd rather hear what he has to say about himself than what you say about him because you complain all the time. At least he gives out compliments."

"But he's complimenting himself!" they said.

Toad grinned. "I'd rather hear compliments all day than complaints. Besides, at least this way I know he's not talking about me when we're not together—the way you talk about him."

And Toad hopped off to meet Fox for a mug of root beer at the little restaurant down the street while the other animals just hurried away to tell their friends about how foolish Toad was.

## The End

Words have the power to heal or harm,
To build or destroy, engage or disarm.
So how will you handle the words that you use?
Growing evil or good? Which one do you choose?

## LEARN FROM SCRIPTURE

There are really several things going on in this story. We can learn something important from Fox, Toad, and from the other animals.

First of all, what can we learn from Fox? What was his problem?

What about the other animals? What problems did they have?

Here's an interesting Bible verse: "The tongue has the power of life and death, and those who love it will eat its fruit" (Prov. 18:21 NIV). What do you think this verse might have to do with this story?

Okay, now let's think about Toad. What positive lesson can we learn from the way he handled the other animals, and his attitude toward Fox? Who can give me three lessons that we can take away from this story?

# END WITH PRAYER

God, keep us from the trap of complaining, gossiping, or saying bad things about people behind their backs. Instead, teach us, like Toad, to find something good even in bad situations. Amen.

# 50

# GETTING AWAY WITH IT

## FIND THIS OBJECT

COOKIES——Eat them while you read the story.

## ASK THESE QUESTIONS

Have you ever tried to get away with something when someone wasn't looking? Who wants to tell what happened? Do you know what it means to get caught "red-handed"? *(If needed, explain the term to them.)* With all that in mind, let me begin today's story.

## BEGIN THE STORY

"Mom's gonna be home any minute!" said Kyle. "Get down from the counter!"

"No, she's not!" said Brianna reaching for the cookie jar their mother had told them to leave alone. Brianna was two years older than Kyle and always seemed to get her way. "Mom had to stop at the store on the way home, and she won't be back for at least half an hour. Now, help me with this chair so I can reach the cupboard."

"We're gonna get in trooouuuble!"

"No, we're not! She'll never find out." And then Brianna glared at her brother. "Unless someone tells her."

"I won't tell," said Kyle.

"You better not, or I just might have to tell her about how the blender broke when you used it as a sprinkler in the yard by taking the lid off, sticking the hose into it, and turning it onto frappe."

"You promised you wouldn't tell!"

"And I won't, as long as you keep your mouth shut."

And so Kyle helped.

And so Brianna reached for the cookie jar.

And so the chair tipped over and the cookie jar fell to the floor and shattered with a great *Crash!*—a sound so loud that neither Kyle nor Brianna heard the car door slam. And neither Kyle nor Brianna noticed their mother walk through the doorway as they were picking up the pieces.

"What's going on here?" she asked.

Brianna gulped. "Uh-oh."

"Um, there's some broken cookie jar stuff on the floor," Kyle said.

"I can see that! How did it get there?"

"Um, gravity?"

"And which of you two introduced my cookie jar to gravity?"

"It was his fault," said Brianna.

"It was her fault," said Kyle.

"Aha," said their mother. "You're both to blame. And you're both grounded." Then she shook her head. "I told you to leave those cookies alone. Now I'll have to bake two dozen more for the PTA meeting tomorrow night. What did you think? That just because I stepped out of the house for a few minutes that you could disobey me?"

"Something like that," said Kyle.

"Kyle broke your blender," said Brianna.

Their mother looked at her quizzically and then sighed. "It's too bad I can't trust you two to be alone together for an hour. I guess I'll have to bring Charlene over to babysit tomorrow."

"Not Charlene!" cried Kyle and Brianna together. "She's the meanest babysitter in the universe!"

"Well, you should have thought of that before you decided to disobey me."

And so, the next evening during the PTA meeting, Charlene came over to babysit and lounged on the couch eating peppermint ice cream while she made Brianna and Kyle do the dishes, sweep the floor, and even clean out the cat's litter box. Because she really was the meanest babysitter in the universe.

## The End

> When the cat's away, the mice will play
> And do what they wouldn't do
> If the cat were there and well aware
> Of catching them in his view.

## LEARN FROM SCRIPTURE

Jesus often warned his followers to be ready for his return in the days leading up to the end of the world. Just because we don't see Jesus physically here with us doesn't mean we should disobey him. *(Read or paraphrase Jesus' parable in Luke 12:42–47. Talk about how it is similar to and different from the story you just read.)*

What do you think Jesus' point is? Sometimes, when we think no one is watching, we try to get away with doing stuff we wouldn't do if people were there watching us.

Often we aren't watchful or careful. Let's strive to live with a joyful expectation of Jesus' return, not fear that he might catch us doing something wrong. And let's be careful to remain watchful and ready.

## END WITH PRAYER

> God, help us not to get tired of waiting for you to return or to think we can get away with stuff just because Jesus doesn't seem to be around. Give us both patience and courage. Amen.

# 51

# THE KING'S INVITATION

## FIND THIS OBJECT

AN INVITATION to a wedding or another special gathering *(Print one out from the Internet if necessary.)*—If desired, make invitations for all of the family members to attend a special dessert celebration after the story—then have a party as a family!

## ASK THESE QUESTIONS

Have you ever been invited to a sleepover or a birthday party? What did you do when you were invited? Did you call your friend back and say you could come?

Now think about this—could you enjoy the cake at a birthday party if you didn't respond to the invitation and you didn't show up at the party? Pay attention to the different ways people respond to the invitations in this story.

## BEGIN THE STORY

One day long ago, the king and the queen sent out invitations to the Queen's Masquerade Ball, the greatest dance in the land! Zip, zip hurrah!

The king's messenger gave invitations to everyone he met. "Come to the Queen's Masquerade Ball, the greatest dance in the land! Zip, zip hurrah!" he would say, and then he would hand them the engraved invitation from the king.

Some people took the invitations and stuffed them into their pockets—way down deep by all the lint and cookie crumbs and loose change—and quickly forgot they were even there.

Those people never made it to the ball.

Others accepted the invitations, but thought, *Hmm, the queen would never invite someone like me to the palace. There must be some mistake.* And so they never even considered going to the Masquerade Ball—Zip, zip hurrah!—and went home instead to their dingy homes to eat stale, cold beet soup.

Other people were thrilled to be invited! After all, they'd been invited to the palace! They quickly framed their invitations and put them above the fireplace to show off to relatives who might visit for warm cider and roast pheasant on weekends in November. But of course, they didn't go to the ball, either.

Only a few people brought their invitations to the palace on the night of the Queen's Masquerade Ball. They handed them to the knights by the drawbridge and were quickly welcomed inside where they feasted with the royal family, danced until dawn, met the king and queen for themselves, and were then able to share the story of that wonderful night with others.

Zip, zip hurrah!

## *The End*

The palace is waiting, the party's prepared.
The drawbridge is lowered, the king has declared
That all who would enter can join in the fun.
Don't stay far away; the ball has begun!

## LEARN FROM SCRIPTURE

Jesus often told stories about God's kingdom. Can you think of which one of his parables this story reminds you of? *(Your children might mention the parable of the sower and the seeds found in Matthew 13:1–9, 18–23, or the story of the feast for the least found in Luke 14:15–24. Whichever they suggest, ask them to tell you why they thought of that story.)*

This fable is similar to a number of Jesus' stories. The King of Kings has indeed invited us to enter his kingdom and dine at his table. Do you know how we do that? *(Allow them to respond.)* There's only one way. It's all through faith in Jesus. As the Bible says, "To all who believed him and accepted him, he gave the right to become children of God. They are reborn! This is not a physical birth resulting from human passion or plan—this rebirth comes from God" (John 1:12–13).

*(If appropriate, invite your children to accept and believe the invitation to enter God's kingdom and become one of his children—then have a party to celebrate!)*

## END WITH PRAYER

God, you have invited us. We ask that you would remove our excuses and hesitations and draw us deeper into your love. Show us our place in your kingdom. Amen.

# 52

# THE TWO TREES

## FIND THIS OBJECT

A TREE——Sit beneath a tree in your yard or on your street while you read this story.

## ASK THESE QUESTIONS

Think about a time when you were jealous of someone. What happened to make you so jealous?

Did being jealous feel good or not so good? Does being jealous make you happier or sadder? Explain what you mean.

What can be done about jealousy? Why do we get jealous of others—because we love them or because we love ourselves? Explain what you mean.

## BEGIN THE STORY

Once upon a time there were two baby trees. Both hoped to one day become Great Trees of the Forest.

One of the trees had bright red buds on her branches, while the other sprouted buds the color of lemonade. And as they grew, they began to call each other by the color of the buds that formed on their leaves—Redbud and Yellowbud.

They grew near an old fencepost by the edge of the forest. One day, a robin landed on the post and called out a sweet morning song. Redbud and Yellowbud watched and listened.

And as she did, Redbud became jealous. "Why doesn't that bird land on my branches?" she asked. "Why won't that bird call out a sweet song while sitting on *me*? It's just not fair!"

But Yellowbud just closed his eyes and listened. "It doesn't matter where the bird sits, Redbud. Let's just enjoy the music!"

As time went by, the bird frequently returned to that fencepost to sing. And each time she listened, Redbud became more and more jealous. She even stuck two of her branches in her ears to block out the song of the bird. It hurt terribly to twist her branches so, but her jealous heart could think of nothing else to do.

Yellowbud just sighed and smiled and listened—and grew. With each passing year, he became straighter and stronger and taller, while Redbud became more and more bent and curled and crooked.

Eventually, Redbud stopped talking to Yellowbud altogether. After all, it was getting harder for her to speak since her mouth and throat were so gnarled. And the branches she'd stuck in her ears had grown thick and made it hard for her to hear.

Yellowbud stretched his branches farther and farther across the field while Redbud began to rot from the inside out.

One day when the farmer came to check his fence he noticed the two trees. *How strange!* he thought. *Such a lovely tree has grown next to such an ugly and knotty one. I ought to cut that rotten one down so it doesn't fall on my fence. And besides, then everyone who passes this way will see that this lovely tree with the yellow buds is one of the Great Trees of the Forest.*

And as he left to fetch his ax, a robin settled into the spreading branches of Yellowbud and began to sing a sweet morning song to the forest.

## The End

Jealousy turns good feelings to bad,
Makes happy hearts heavy and heavy hearts sad.
So when you feel jealous, change your attitude quick.
Or your happy heart just might turn ugly and sick.

# LEARN FROM SCRIPTURE

When we become jealous of others, we end up hurting ourselves. Proverbs 14:30 says, "A relaxed attitude lengthens life; jealousy rots it away." How does jealousy rot us away? Why is it hard to love people you're jealous of?

*(Take a few minutes to discuss envy, jealousy, and coveting—envy is when we want someone else's position in life, jealousy is when we want someone else's attention or affection, and coveting is when we want someone else's stuff.)*

In his letter to Timothy, Paul wrote that "godliness with contentment is great gain" (1 Tim. 6:6 NIV). What do you think he meant by that? Describe what it means to be content. What does it mean to be godly? What do *you* think the secret to true contentment is? *(Hint: In Philippians 4:11–12 Paul said he learned the secret to true contentment. Look it up. What did he write?)*

# END WITH PRAYER

God, teach us to be content. Jealousy eats away at our joy. Forgive us for the times we've been jealous and teach us to be thankful to you instead. Remind us of all the kind things you do for us every day. Amen.

# 53

# THE MEADOW

## FIND THIS OBJECT

A PEACEFUL PLACE OUTDOORS——If desired, read this devotion outside in your yard or in a nearby meadow, tree house, or other special place.

## ASK THESE QUESTIONS

We all need a quiet place where we can get away from our problems and where we can dream, talk to God, and relax. Do you have a special place or secret place you like to go? What makes it special to you? Why do you go there? Today's story is about just such a place.

## BEGIN THE STORY

A small forest grew on the edge of the city near a yellow house. In the forest was a sheltered meadow filled with flowers and surrounded by trees. And it was there in the meadow that the sisters played.

On some days the girls pretended to be mothers and the meadow became their home. "This is my house," said one of the girls. "And here are my children!" And she laid out a line of five daises on soft, leafy beds.

On other days the meadow became a palace, and the girls were princesses. And sometimes it was a cabin on the frontier, and the girls were watching for Mohicans riding through the pines. And sometimes the meadow was a hospital, and all the flowers were patients.

"Come in, girls!" called their mother from the house when it started to get dark. "It's time for bed!"

And the girls would pretend not to hear her, and giggle and squeal as girls do, and talk in girly voices about how they would stay there in the meadow forever.

"Girls!"

"Oh, all right, Mother! We're coming!"

Then, they would say goodnight to their flowery children and tuck them into their leafy beds, and head back to the house. All summer and into the fall the girls returned to the meadow whenever they could, and that made the meadow very happy.

The seasons passed with the years. Autumn gave way to winter; winter gave birth to spring. And the meadow waited for the girls. But then came the year that a truck pulled up to the house. After packing the truck with boxes and furniture, the girls left for a new home.

So the quiet meadow waited and waited, and grew greener and thicker, and more and more forgotten. But it didn't forget the girls. It remembered all of their adventures together. And sometimes it played pretend without the girls, but it just wasn't the same.

Time passed. Years and seasons faded, until one day a truck returned and two men began to unload boxes and furniture. The meadow heard footsteps. Then a woman and two young girls appeared at the edge of the trees.

"This is where my castle was!" the woman cried. "It looks different now, but the same, too! And that's where we watched for Indians!"

And her daughters' eyes glistened. "We see them!" they cried, for they understood those kinds of things. And so, as a new summer grew around them, the girls played in that meadow just as their mother had done. And that night the meadow heard familiar words, "Come in, girls! It's time for bed!"

And the meadow heard familiar giggles, too.

"Oh, all right! We're coming!"

And then the girls said goodnight to their children and tucked them into their leafy beds and headed back to the house.

And as they left, the stars glistened high above the dreams of tomorrow.

## *The End*

> Days and seasons pass away,
> Grown-ups dream and children play.
> And often the real and possible blend
> In the laughter of childhood
> In that place called pretend.

## LEARN FROM SCRIPTURE

*(This story is really about a lot of things—growing up, families, change, and imagination. You could lead a discussion about any one of them. One application could be that change in life is normal—growing up and getting old is all a part of God's plan: "There is a time for everything," wrote Solomon, "a season for every activity under heaven. A time to be born and a time to die. A time to plant and a time to harvest" [Eccl. 3:1–2]).* Discuss why it's hard to pass from one season to another. What holds us back? Are these good reasons or not? What season is closing in your life? Which one is opening?

## END WITH PRAYER

*(Have the children lead the prayer. Invite them to pray that as we get older, our faith will get younger. Encourage them to pray in their own words, since those are usually the most heartfelt prayers of all.)*

# 54

# THE PORCUPINE WHO WORRIED TOO MUCH

## FIND THIS OBJECT

A HAIR BRUSH——Flip the brush bristles-side up on the table.

## ASK THESE QUESTIONS

What animal does this hair brush remind you of?

*(Affirm their answers. If none of them suggest a porcupine, offer that as your idea.)*

Today's story is about a porcupine with a problem.

## BEGIN THE STORY

Jasmine the Porcupine would worry about everything. She worried about trees falling on her head whenever she walked through the forest. She worried that her breakfast food would be poisoned by the weasel family, who just didn't seem to like her. And then after eating breakfast and not dying from poison, she worried that maybe it was the slow-acting kind of poison and that she'd keel over dead right in the middle of her morning tai chi workout. She even worried about whether or not aliens would abduct her and do strange experiments on her brain.

Jasmine worried way too much.

One day when she was near the berry patch she saw a bear in the path. *Oh, no! He'll probably eat me!* she thought. *Or maybe take me prisoner in his cave and feed me nothing but tofu and lilies and never let me see the light of day again!*

"Hi," said the bear.

"Don't do it!" cried Jasmine. "I can't stand tofu!"

The bear looked at her in a confused sort of a way, and then backed away from her very slowly.

As Jasmine watched him leave, she thought, *Oh, no! He's probably going to get his friends and they're going to capture me and cook me alive, boiling me in a giant vat of bread pudding!*

"Help!" she yelled, looking around wildly at the forest, searching for bears. "They're out to get me! Keep the pudding far away! Keep the pudding far away!"

When she didn't see any bears, she thought it was probably because they were all hiding in her house, in the cupboards and drawers, and underneath the nightstand beside her bed. *They probably drank some shrinking potion!* she thought. *And as soon as I walk through the door, they'll grow big again and take me away!*

One day Jasmine's friend, Erik the Groundhog, suggested that she write down her worries. "You have such an incredible imagination!" he said. "Don't let it go to waste!"

And so that's exactly what Jasmine did. Whenever she worried about something, she would turn it into a story. And in time she became a famous novelist. Her books have been translated into sixteen languages and sell well all over the world, especially in France where, for some unknown reason, the people are especially drawn to the idea of a creative porcupine.

## The End

Take a careful look at your life
And be ready for a surprise.
What seems to be your biggest flaw
Could be a blessing in disguise.

# LEARN FROM SCRIPTURE

Really, this story can teach us lessons both about worry and about how we handle our problems or weaknesses. Is worry a good thing? Jesus told his followers not to worry, but just to seek God's will and God's ways today. (See Matthew 6:25–34.)

So that's the first lesson. Now think about Erik. How did he help Jasmine? Are there ways you could help someone find a way to turn a weakness into a strength?

# END WITH PRAYER

Jesus, the more we trust in you, the less we need to worry about life. So help us to trust you. Also, help us to find the areas of our lives where we have weaknesses and show us how to turn those areas into strengths. Thanks. Amen.

# 55

# RITA'S DANCE

## FIND THIS OBJECT

A CHAIR——Push your chairs away from the table and ask your children to imagine what it would be like to be in a wheelchair all the time.

## ASK THESE QUESTIONS

*(Explain that sometimes in our world accidents happen that cause people to lose the ability to do the things they used to do—running, hearing, walking, seeing, or thinking the same as before.)* Can you think of anyone you know who that has happened to?

What would you do for fun if you couldn't walk around but had to stay in a wheelchair all day? Could you still find ways to do the things you enjoy? In today's story, a girl named Rita has to figure out how to respond when an accident happens to her.

## BEGIN THE STORY

Before the accident, Rita used to run and jump and skip and dance in the park among the aspen trees.

But now, she just stared through the hospital windows and only remembered those days—laughing and twirling, spinning and leaping, swinging her arms and kicking her feet up high toward the blue summer sky.

"Soon you'll be able to visit the park again," the doctors told her. "But Rita, it'll be a long time before you can walk and run again. It might be until forever."

So Rita sat by the window in her wheelchair, watching her friends play—skipping and running and dancing in the park by the aspen trees—wishing she could join them.

Then two months after the accident, Rita finally left the hospital. Her mother pushed her wheelchair to the place where the aspens stood with their golden autumn leaves.

Rita saw the leaves quiver and shake in the afternoon breeze. They seemed to dance in the daylight.

And Rita had an idea.

Her mother asked her, "Do you remember when you used to come here to dance?"

"Yes," said Rita. "And today I'll dance again."

"But Rita, how can you dance? Your legs don't work like they used to."

"My legs were only a small part of my dance," replied Rita softly. "Watch me dance like the trees!"

Then Rita raised her arms. She wiggled her hands and closed her eyes and felt the breeze trail through her fingers. "See my branches!" she said to her mother. Then she began to sway her arms and wave her fingers in the afternoon sun as the leaves swirled down around her. And that day, the trees were not the only ones to dance in the swirl of autumn leaves.

## The End

Bad times will come. We all know it's true,
But how will you act when they happen to you?
Will you give up and get angry or perhaps take the chance
That God will teach you a new way to dance?

## LEARN FROM SCRIPTURE

Sometimes good things happen to us, and sometimes bad things happen. It's a part of life we have no control over. What we do have control over is how we respond to the events that come our way. We can control our attitude. And when we trust God through the tough times, God gives us an opportunity for joy. As James wrote, "Dear brothers and sisters, whenever trouble comes your way, let it be an opportunity for joy. For when your faith is tested, your endurance has a chance to grow. So let it grow, for when your endurance is fully developed, you will be strong in character and ready for anything" (James 1:2–4).

The road to a stronger character isn't an easy one. When trouble comes, God can teach us new ways to dance if only we stay open to his joy. Let's pray a dancing prayer tonight!

## END WITH PRAYER

*(Do a dancing prayer. Wave your arms or fingers and praise God for being loving, powerful, and in charge of making good come out of even bad circumstances.)*

God, teach us new ways to dance when troubles come into our lives! Amen.

# 56

# THE WRONG TRACK

## FIND THIS OBJECT

A TOY RAILROAD CAR or a picture of a roller coaster—You may want to have your children help you search the Internet and then print a picture of a favorite roller coaster from a theme park you've visited.

## ASK THESE QUESTIONS

Do you ever get bored with the things you have to do every day? What do you do when you get bored? What are the things that bore you the most?

These days there are so many movies to watch, video games to play, books to read, songs to listen to, games to play, and of course, homework assignments to do. So, why are people today more bored than ever before? Why do you think so few people are truly happy? As I read this story, think about your life. Think about the things that bore you and the things that leave you truly amazed.

## BEGIN THE STORY

Wendy the Ferris Wheel was amazed every time she left the ground. There were always different people riding in her baskets, and the clouds high above her in the sky were always changing. Sometimes, when the day was especially clear, she could almost see to the next county!

"Life is so exciting!" she said.

But nearby her at the amusement park, Bitzy the Roller Coaster was neither happy nor excited. Every day she saw the same sights Wendy did, but in a different way. Every day she went around her track taking boys and girls and moms and dads (and an occasional grandma and grandpa) high then low, then around the bend, then upside down and on a twisty twirl. But she was sooooo bored.

"All I ever do is follow the same dumb track all day long!" she whined. "Just the same thing over and over all day every day! Life is so boring!"

Oh, sure, for a while it had been fun, back when she was newly built ten years ago, but not anymore. All she wanted was a little adventure! From the top of her highest hill, Bitzy could see a train and hear his whistle as he raced through the countryside. *Oh, if only I were a train!* she thought. *Then I'd be free to explore the world! I could see new things and visit faraway cities! Then I would be happy!*

But little did she know that every time Larry the Train Engine chugged past the amusement park he would sigh to himself. "Life is so dull," he'd say. "If only I were a roller coaster! My life is so boring—always going straight ahead! Always going forward, forward, forward! If only I were a roller coaster, then at least I could go high then low, then around the bend, then upside down and on a twisty twirl!"

Well, God heard everything Larry, Wendy, and Bitzy said, and he decided to give all three of them what they wanted most. "But if I change things around, you won't be able to switch back," he told them. "If I switch you around, you'll be switched forever."

"Oh, we don't care!" said Bitzy. "Make me into a train!"

"Neither do I!" cried Larry. "Make me a roller coaster!"

"I'd like to stay just as I am," said Wendy. "Will that be okay?"

"Sure, Wendy," said God. "I was hoping you'd say that."

So Bitzy became a train and Larry became a roller coaster, and Wendy remained just as she was. And pretty soon, Bitzy and Larry were just as bored as they'd ever been, while Wendy the Ferris Wheel continued to be amazed at the world every time her baskets left the ground.

## *The End*

Wishing you were someone else
Will make you sad and quite resentful—
But enjoying your life as a gift from God
Will help you to always be contentful.

## LEARN FROM SCRIPTURE

Sometimes when we see other people's gifts or their place in life we think we'd be happier if only we were like them. Has that ever happened to you? Let's think about that for a minute. Is the problem usually about what you have to do or your attitude about what you have to do?

Long ago a man searched all over for happiness and finally, he wrote, "To enjoy your work and accept your lot in life—that is indeed a gift from God" (Eccl. 5:19).

It's easy to think we'd be happier living someone else's life, but God wants us to stop looking for happiness out there somewhere and find joy in the life and work he's given each of us to do. Then we can be more like Wendy and less like Larry and Bitzy.

## END WITH PRAYER

God, remind us that this day, this moment, is a gift from you. Remind us that you want us to enjoy our lives. Forgive us for the times we've envied other people's lives and been bored with our own. Help us to be content with whatever we have and become more amazed at the world every time we open our eyes. Amen.

# 57

# WHEN GOD'S DREAM CAME TRUE

## FIND THIS OBJECT

A HANDHELD MIRROR——Hide the mirror on your lap before you begin. You'll pull it out as a surprise later in the story. You'll probably want to read through this story first before reading it aloud to your family, so that you can become familiar with when to hold up the mirror.

## ASK THESE QUESTIONS

*(You may wish to talk about how different each one of us is. We each have different fingerprints, laughter, interests, taste buds, and even different patterns on the tops of our tongues! Discuss why you think that is.)*

Do you ever wonder why God made you the way he did? Why do you think you are just that size, shape, and color? I used to wonder. After all, there are so many people faster and stronger and smarter and funnier than me. Why did God make me the way he did? Sometimes I thought maybe God made a mistake when he was making me. But then, one day, someone told me about God's dream …

# BEGIN THE STORY

Long ago, before the world was even made, God had a dream. God dreamed he was no longer alone. He dreamed of talking and playing and laughing with someone he could call his friend. God dreamed of a friend who would stay close by him forever. The dream made God so happy he decided to make it come true.

Since God loves to imagine the impossible, he wanted a friend who could do the same. *I'll create a dreamer, just like me*, thought God. *And since I love music, I'll give my friend a special song that can only be heard in the still of the morning. Someday we'll sing it together!*

So, God poured many dreams and many songs into his friend.

*How can our friendship always grow stronger?* wondered God. *I know! I'll put an empty place in my friend's heart that I can fill slowly, day by day, with love. That way, I'll be able to grow my friend's joy a little at a time, forever.*

So, God gave his friend the gift of an empty heart that longed to be filled.

*My friend must be able both to laugh and to cry, just like me. My friend must be able to feel joy and sadness, wonder and surprise, peace and trust, and hope. And I will let my friend love. Just like me. I'll even let my friend feel pain. Just like me. Then, whenever my friend hurts, I'll be there to share the pain and take it away. After all, that's what friends are for.*

So, God added tears and giggles and a whole heap of love to the friend he was creating. God gave his friend eyes that could twinkle, legs that could dance, and arms that could swing and lift and hug. And God tossed a little sunlight into the soul of his friend, just for good measure.

*What else? ... What else? ...* thought God. *We'll have so many special moments together! If only we could relive them again and again ... Yes! I'll give my friend a memory! Let there be memory inside of my friend!*

Then, God filled his friend with the freedom of the wind that tickles your hair, the stillness of moonbeams reflecting off the water, and the playfulness of a mountain stream rushing toward the sea. *It'll be fun playing with this kind of friend!* thought God.

God's friend was taking shape, but God wasn't finished yet.

*I'll give my friend a mind to know me, a heart to love me, and a will to find me. And most of all, my friend must love stories, just like me.* So God made his friend hungry for stories.

God doesn't like easy answers, so he filled his friend with questions. *This way my friend will enjoy the mysteries of life,* thought God.

And God decided to remain a mystery himself. *I'll sprinkle clues of myself all around my friend to show that I'm here. Then my friend will always know I'm nearby but will keep looking for me. It'll be an adventure as we search for each other ... And, oh! When we finally meet! I'll make that the best day of my friend's life! Yes! I'll stay close, but just out of sight. That way, my friend can learn faith, the most important lesson of all.*

So God let glimpses of himself shine into the world. And he decided to whisper where he was rather than shout, so his friend would learn how to listen.

And because God has a sense of humor, he added eyebrows, dimples, and a belly button. Then God laughed. His friend was almost done.

Finally, God decided, *I'll make my friend different from anything else I've ever made. My friend is that special to me.* So, God searched all throughout his imagination to find just the right shape and size for his friend. He explored all the way to the end of the rainbow to find just the right color hair and skin and toenails for his friend. He chose the perfect ears and taste buds and toes. And he took his time. After all, God was creating a masterpiece.

And when God was finished creating his dream he looked down from heaven and smiled ... *(As you say these next two words, pull out the hand mirror and hold it out so your children can see their reflection in it.)* at you.

That's right, you are a dream come true. You are the friend God has always wanted! You were created to be with God forever. You are a masterpiece.

The next time you wonder why God made you the way he did, remember it wasn't a mistake. You are the child of a dream that grew in the heart of God! A dream God fell in love with, a dream that made him so happy he decided to make *you* come true.

## The End

God's love is so great, and God's love is so grand,
That he made people different all over the land.
He wants us to know him and be close till the end.
That's what God's really like—
Yes, he's that kind of friend.

# LEARN FROM SCRIPTURE

The Bible explains that God dreamed of you even before he shaped the planets or whispered out the world. Listen to these words from the Bible: "Long ago, even before he made the world, God loved us and chose us in Christ to be holy and without fault in his eyes. His unchanging plan has always been to adopt us into his own family by bringing us to himself through Jesus Christ. And this gave him great pleasure" (Eph. 1:4–5). When God dreamed of you, it gave him great pleasure. And the day you believe in him will bring him the most pleasure of all.

*(Take a little time to talk more about believing in God [faith], the bad things we do that separate us from being close to him [sin], and how we can receive God's forgiveness [confession].)*

# END WITH PRAYER

God, remind us how much we matter to you. Remind us each how special we are, how unique you made us. We know that you long to be friends with us. Help us to show that we're friends with you by the things we believe and the things that we do. Amen.

# SUBJECT INDEX

# NOTES

1. Readers familiar with Aesop's fables will see some similarities between the first half of this story and Aesop's fable of "The Wolf and the Kid." I like how they teach different truths even though the two stories have a similar starting place.
2. One time I heard someone say, "If only the most beautiful birds would sing, the forest would be a quiet place indeed." I thought that was wonderful and decided to write a story that would reinforce the moral.
3. This poem first appeared on my audio CD, "The Genetically Altered Nine-Foot-Tall Killer Mutant Chicken (And Other Kid-sized Stories)" and is used here with my permission. This CD is available on my Web site: www.stevenjames.net.
4. Based on Ecclesiastes 9:13–16.
5. I based this fable on a story I heard about an overweight man imprisoned in a room. All he had to do was lose weight and he could leave. I tell that story in my book *Story: Recapture the Mystery* (Revell, 2006) on pages 53–54. I'm not sure where the original plot might be from, but it has stuck with me over the years.
6. This story first appeared on my audio CD, "The Genetically Altered Nine-Foot-Tall Killer Mutant Chicken (And Other Kid-sized Stories)" and is used here with my permission. This CD is available on my Web site: www.stevenjames.net.
7. In the late 1990s I met a man named Sergei who grew up in the part of the former Soviet Union now known as Georgia. He told me this story and mentioned that it was a Georgian folktale. I've never seen it in a collection of stories before, so I thought I would share it here.
8. One time, nearly ten years ago when I was speaking at a church, a boy came up to me and told me this story. I've never been able to track down the source of the story nor have I ever seen it appear in print before. So, here it is. All credit goes to the unknown author.